Rock & Roll DINER

| Popular
American Cooking | Classic
Rock & Roll Music |

OTHER BOOKS IN THE MENUS AND MUSIC SERIES

Dinner and Dessert

Holidays

Dinners for Two

Nutcracker Sweet

Music and Food of Spain

Picnics

Dining and the Opera in Manhattan

Lighthearted Gourmet

Romance

Sharon O'Connor's Menus and Music

Rock & Roll DINER

| Popular American Cooking | Classic Rock & Roll Music |

Menus and Music Productions, Inc.
Emeryville, California

Library of Congress Cataloging-in-Publication Data
O'Connor, Sharon
Menus and Music Volume X
Rock & Roll Diner
Popular American Cooking
Classic Rock & Roll Music

Includes Index
1. Cookery 2. Entertaining
I. Title
96-76188

ISBN 1-883914-13-2 (paperback)
ISBN 1-883914-12-4 (hardcover)

Menus and Music Productions, Inc.
1462 66th Street
Emeryville, CA 94608
(510) 658-9100

Jeanie Tracy appears courtesy of Pulse-8 Records, London

Bette's Oceanview Diner recipe on page 43 is from *The Pancake Handbook* by Stephen
Siegelman, Sue Conley, and Bette Kroening. Published by Ten Speed Press, Berkeley,
1994

Book and cover design by Michael Osborne Design, Inc.
Cover photograph of Max's Diner, San Francisco, by Mark McLane
Food styling by Danielle Di Salvo

Manufactured in the United States of America
10 9 8 7 6 5 4 3 2 1

CONTENTS

INTRODUCTION

Jukebox-jolted diners shake, rattle, and roll across America and are known for their good food and good times!

The recipes included here have pleased diner customers from coast to coast. Now you can enjoy a cook's road trip by preparing Jambalaya from New Orleans, Five-Way Chili from Cincinnati, Seafood Chowder from Maine, and Spinach Quesadillas with Avocado Salsa from California. You'll love serving this simple, satisfying food at home.

While you might not be able to re-create the gleam of stainless steel or the ongoing banter of the diner, these authentic recipes will give you a taste of traditional and contemporary American cooking that's ideal fare for family meals and casual dinner parties. Most of the recipes were created by talented cooks rather than trained chefs, and their popular home-style dishes are delicious! After all, even brilliant chefs cook homey dishes for themselves or old friends and grow dreamy-eyed when they say, "You should have known my mother's cooking . . ."

People love the variety found on diner menus, which can be eight pages long with a page or two of daily specials. Diners are quite the opposite of fast-food franchises, with their corporate standardization and emphasis on convenience items. Although diners are an American institution and cling to an old-fashioned look, they do make concessions to changing food tastes. Some of the recipes in the book, such as those for meat loaf, Yankee pot roast, and apple pie, are evocatively tied to the past, but today's diner menus also feature more chicken and fish, fresh vegetables from local farms, and innovative dishes such as Thai Peanut Soup, Blackened Chicken with Red Pepper Sauce, Poached Pears in Wine, and Crème Brûlée.

More than just providing nostalgic architecture and "comfort" food, diners are often the social hub of their community. Customers are known by name, community events and local service announcements are posted by the cash register, and people from all walks of life end up eating at the counter and discussing politics or local gossip. Meals are served by waitresses who know which customers like their coffee black, the follies of the local children, the successes of the grandchildren, and the outcome of a surgery or a daughter's piano recital. Even before a regular settles onto a stool, the waitress can call in an order for a "BLT with mayo." As havens of humanity, diners help cultivate relationships and keep a colder society at bay. And diner jukeboxes keep millions of customers entertained while they wait for their orders.

The classic rock & roll music recorded for this volume will set the stage for some good times. You'll hear songs—like "My Girl," "Shake Rattle and Roll," and "Blueberry Hill"—by some of the pioneers of rock & roll that will thrill you to the marrow no matter when you first heard them. I brought together top San Francisco Bay Area musicians to record some of the jukebox hits they grew up on. Long days in the studio were spent recording vocalists and instrumentalists playing the guitar, drums, bass, piano, organ, violin, cello, trumpet, and tenor, alto, and baritone saxophones. During the sessions, everyone had a tremendous amount of fun, and I hope you'll be able to hear that! As for myself, I'll remember the experience always.

So go ahead and enjoy making some of this good food for yourself. Use the best-quality, freshest ingredients available to re-create an entire menu, or choose dishes from several places to create your own sampler. Fire up your stove and fill your home with the delicious aroma of home-cooked food and the clatter of dishes and silverware. Turn up the music and have some fun!

—*Sharon O'Connor*

A HISTORY OF THE DINER

Diner history began in 1872, when Walter Scott drove a horse-drawn freight wagon filled with sandwiches, boiled eggs, buttered bread, pies, and coffee down Westminster Street in Providence, Rhode Island. Late-night factory workers couldn't purchase anything to eat after 8 p.m., when all the restaurants in town closed for the evening, so the enterprising Scott brought the food *to* his hungry customers.

Twelve years later, Samuel Jones noticed some lunch wagon customers standing outside in the rain eating and had an inspiration: he would build a lunch cart big enough for people to come inside. In 1887, at the New England Fair in Worcester, Massachusetts, for the first time ever customers entered a lunch cart on wheels. Jones's cart had a kitchen, fancy woodwork, stained glass windows, standing room for customers, and a menu that included sand- wiches, pie, cake, milk, and coffee. The idea of eating inside a lunch cart was an instant success.

Lunch wagons were soon being mass-produced by Thomas H. Buckley, who became known as the "Lunch Wagon King." By 1892, Buckley's firm, the New England Night Lunch Wagon Company, had built more than seventy-five wagons that were models of efficiency. Several were sold to the Church Temperance Society in New York City and were endowed by prominent New Yorkers, including Cornelius Vanderbilt, because they offered stiff competition to the free lunch that most New York bars provided during the 1890s. It was

Buckley's idea to add cooking stoves to his lunch wagons, which allowed for expanded menus. A typical New England menu included sandwiches, frankfurters, hamburgers, pork and beans, corned beef, beef stew, clam chowder, waffles, boiled eggs, doughnuts, pies, and coffee.

These first lunch wagons underwent many changes while evolving into the roadside diners of the twentieth century. At the turn of the century, they were so popular that the city of Providence, Rhode Island, had nearly fifty wagons roaming its streets by 1912. At the same time, street railway companies were beginning to electrify, and discarded horsecars were quickly and cheaply converted to mobile eateries. Many of the discarded trolley cars and aging first-generation lunch wagons were eyesores, however, and the subject of citizen complaints. Wagon owners soon found it easier to rent a good site off the road and set up their wagons as permanent restaurants in order to become immune from rulings levelled against mobile eateries.

In 1905, Patrick J. "Pop" Tierney entered the diner manufacturing business and built so many good ones that he restored the lunch car to its lost respectability. His miniature restaurants were approximately thirty feet long and ten feet wide, so they could still be shipped by railway to distant sites. By 1917, Tierney's shop was turning out a lunch car a day, and the business was transformed from a practical novelty to an American institution.

Sometime between 1923 and 1924, the lunch car became a "diner." In 1922, diner manufacturer Jerry O'Mahony's catalog pictured "lunch cars"; two years later, it showed many models called "diners." This new name linked them with the fine dining experience offered on Pullman trains, and it also better described the expanded fare of breakfast, lunch, and dinner available twenty-four hours a day. During the 1920s, most diners were still located in cities near retail districts, traffic centers, theaters, and factories, but they were also beginning to appear in small towns and along the new highways built to serve automobile drivers. People liked the camaraderie, the banter, the counter showmanship, and, of course, the food. Placing an emphasis on cleanliness and ease of operation, most diners had a long marble counter, a steam table, a gas stove, a grill, iceboxes, dessert display cases, coffee urns, and an exhaust hood of German silver, an alloy that was the precursor to stainless steel. Tile floors and white tile walls were popular, and the stools were typically made of white porcelain enamel, sometimes topped with wooden or leather seats.

Until the mid-1920s, most women would not set foot inside a diner because their early days as late-night lunch carts gave them the reputation of being for men only. Now the owners realized they were missing out on an opportunity for more customers and began working to attract women. "Ladies Invited" signs appeared, flower boxes, shrubs, and frosted glass were added, and menus began featuring attractive salads. This bid for more female customers also led to a major design innovation. Because most women didn't feel comfortable perched on counter stools, manufacturers began to offer diners with table or booth service. By the end of the decade, diners were regarded as inexpensive, respectable places to eat, and this reputation served them well during the 1930s.

The decade following the stock-market crash of 1929 saw many changes in the diner industry. Only one major diner manufacturer closed his shop during the Great Depression, and diners were often described as Depression-proof businesses. Everyone still had to eat, and diners offered inexpensive meals for customers and the low overhead required to make a profit for owners. There was a boom in

Blue Plate Special

During the Great Depression of the 1930s, a pottery manufacturer started making plates with separate sections for each part of the meal. At first, for some reason, the plates were only available in blue, but because they were inexpensive and saved on dishwashing, diners started using them for their low-priced daily specials. Other colors eventually became available, but the name stuck.

reconditioned diners for those with limited capital. The Depression years brought about a return to the early days of the dining cars: one-man operation with a limited menu made sense during those tough times, and the increased demand for small units lead to the creation of "dinettes." By 1937, more than a million people a day were eating diner staples such as "angels on horseback" (bacon-wrapped oysters on toast) and "bossy on a board" (roast beef on toast).

A History of the Diner

As the country came out of the Depression, people were interested in moving forward into the future. Industrial designers gave a futuristic look to almost every product, and diner manufacturers were no exception. A sleek new look replaced the hard-edged box design of the 1920s-style diners, and by the end of the 1930s, diner surfaces were brushed, polished, rounded, and wrapped. Designs mimicking the sleek locomotives that symbolized the era were epitomized by the Sterling Streamliner, a diner with one or two bullet-shaped ends, and the Worcester, a diner with slanted rather than rounded ends to give the illusion of mobility. All diner designs were affected by the concept of streamlining—it was synonymous with modernization.

The 1930s saw the introduction of new construction materials such as Formica, glass blocks, and stainless steel. Chosen for longevity, these new materials also helped to convey the ideas of cleanliness and machine-age efficiency. The combination of stainless steel with porcelain enamel produced some of the most eye-catching, colorful diners of all time. Major diner builders of the era included Paramount Diners, Kullman, Worcester, Sterling, and Fodero.

Diners reached the height of their popularity just before and after World War II. The war itself brought an important change to the business: women began working in diners in large numbers. They were needed there just as they were needed in industry to help replace lost manpower, and the diner

The Victor Mug

The Victor mug is so closely associated with diners that it's often called the "diner mug." It was manufactured in the small village of Victor, New York, by a company that originally made insulators and electrical supplies. During World War II, the company's production slowed down, so it began to produce a mug made of insulator porcelain. The mug, which didn't have a handle, was so heavy it didn't slide or tip. This made it perfect for use at sea, giving it its name, the Victor Navy mug. After the war, Buffalo China asked Victor to create a mug with a handle, and the Victor mug was born. Coffee served in these mugs stays hotter longer, and hands aren't scalded because the mugs are basically insulators with handles. The production of Victor mugs stopped in 1991 due to competition from lower-priced diner-style mugs manufactured outside the United States.

A History of the Diner

waitress became an institution. During the war, the production of new diners came to a virtual standstill because of the depleted work force and the government confiscation of steel, copper, and other essentials needed for construction.

When the war ended, the demand for diners was greater than ever. Returning vets wanted small diners to invest in, and as life got back to normal and prices came down, more people began to eat out. The postwar models were fluid-looking structures with no hard edges. All corners were rounded, sometimes even those of the windows. Expensive materials such as marble, mahogany, and leather were rarely used. Most new interiors used plenty of Formica, and booths were framed in chrome and upholstered with Naugahyde. Ninety percent of the cars served customers at tables and booths as well as at the counter.

The boom in families during the 1950s caused many diners to expand in size to handle crowds. In 1957, the new Windmill Diner in Providence, Rhode Island, was a gigantic 150 feet long and 35 feet wide. Many owners worried about being out of date and traded in their old diners for newer designs. The short-order cook was moved behind closed doors to a kitchen annex in the back, and tile floors became a thing of the past, replaced by terrazzo. Interior color schemes were based on a pastel palette rather than the primary colors of earlier years, and in 1950 the Skylark pattern—better known as the "boomerang"—was introduced by Formica.

Formica

Formica-brand laminate was invented in 1913 by Herbert A. Faber and Daniel J. O'Conor. The name of the material comes from "for mica," that is, used in place of mica, and it was first used to insulate industrial products from oils and acids. Formica found its way into diners in the mid-1930s, when new production techniques made it less expensive and more durable. The Paramount Diner company, one of the first manufacturers to use Formica, used it to replace wood, porcelain enamel, and metal in their diners. When a cigarette-proof Formica became available, it was the material of choice for diner countertops, and by 1940 there was a choice of more than seventy Formica colors.

A History of the Diner

During the 1960s, about five thousand roadside diners were still in business. Their distinctive appearance, generous servings of home-style food, and reasonable prices had earned them a place in the heart of the public. As always, new materials were showcased by diner manufacturers. Beach-pebble marble imported from Italy, bamboo curtains, and light fixtures that looked like little flying saucers were common. At the same time, some builders looked to the past for ideas, and the popular colonial-style diner hit the roadside. This conservative design featured exterior walls faced with bricks salvaged from old colonial houses and served to distinguish diners from fast-food restaurants, which were flashy and colorful. With the urban-renewal projects in the early 1960s came city planning boards, which began to legislate "taste" in buildings. In some regions, all new diners had to conform to stringent regulations that often banned stainless-steel buildings and sometimes even the word diner. Several diner builders dropped diner from their names: Paramount Diners became Paramount Modular Concepts, and Kullman Dining Car Company became Kullman Industries.

In 1962, McDonald's ran their first national advertisement in *Life* magazine, and by the end of 1962 the seven-hundred-millionth hamburger was sold. The predictability of the fast-food chains caused a slide in the diner business. In an effort to slow the loss of business, diners cultivated the image of conservative family-oriented places with ever-larger menus, sometimes offering hundreds of food choices from several nationalities. Unlike fast-food franchisers, diner owners still put their imprint on the food, the decor, and even the conversation with their presence.

In the 1960 and 1970s, the trend both in the building of new diners and the renovation of older models was to make a diner look less like a diner.

Jukeboxes and Wall Boxes

Jukeboxes and diners belong together like ham and eggs. Miniature jukeboxes mounted on the wall at booths are known as "wall boxes" in the business and are a great addition to the diner experience. Major manufacturers include AMI, Rockola, Seeburg, and Wurlitzer. Drop in a quarter and you get to hear not only your favorite songs, but everyone else's as well.

Older diners were converted to "restaurants" by such changes as pulling down stainless steel facades, altering windows, refacing walls with brick or stone, and capping buildings off with a Spanish quarry tile mansard roof. The Mediterranean style, with rows of repetitive arches and a stucco exterior, became quite popular.

The 1982 movie *Diner* inspired a resurgence of diner mania. The media was saturated with diner articles and features, and the diner image provided the jumping-off point for many restaurants in the 1980s and on into the 1990s. This attention led to the creation of *new* old-style diners, and it was also good for older original diners; fewer of them are being demolished today because of a greater awareness and appreciation of this unique dining experience.

Now, in the 1990s, diners are flourishing across the United States, from nostalgic prefabricated booth-and-countertop models to custom-designed spots that seat hundreds and gross millions. Colonial- and Mediterranean-style places are being redone with less stone and brick and more polished granite, marble, glass, and stainless steel. New versions of classic 1940s- and 1950s-style diners are being re-created, and older diners are being nominated to the National Register of Historic Places. Menus across the country are diverse and include traditional diner fare as well as more eclectic and regional selections.

Today, eating at a diner is an experience that most Americans relish, whether they go regularly or just once in a while. These familiar eating places are a part of American culture and reflect our energy, language, tempo, and style. Long may they last.

A History of the Diner

DINER TALK

The rapid-fire recitation of short-order code by cooks, waitresses, and waiters is a part of the American vernacular enjoyed by diner staff and customers of all ages and backgrounds. I hope the following sampling will add to your own enjoyment.

Adam and Eve on a raft: two poached eggs on toast

Adam's Ale: water

All hot: baked potato

Angels on horseback: oysters rolled in bacon and served on toast

Atlanta special: Coca-Cola

Baled hay: shredded wheat

Balloon juice: seltzer water

B and B: bread and butter

Beef stick: bone

Belly furniture: food

Biddy board: French toast

Black and white: chocolate soda with vanilla ice cream

Black cow: chocolate milk

Blowout patches: pancakes

Boiled leaves: tea

Break it and shake it: add egg to a drink

Canned cow: evaporated milk

Chicago: pineapple sundae

Chokies: artichokes

C. J. White: cream cheese and jelly sandwich on white bread

Cowboy with spurs: Western omelet with French fries

Cow paste: butter

Cremate it: toast the bread

Dough well done with cow to cover: buttered toast

Drag one through Georgia: Pepsi with chocolate syrup

Flop two: two fried eggs, over easy

Fry two, let the sun shine: fry two eggs with yolks unbroken

Georgia pie: peach pie

Guess water: soup

Hen fruit: egg

Hoboken special: pineapple soda with chocolate ice cream

Hold the grass: a sandwich without lettuce

Hope: oatmeal

Hot one: bowl of chili

Hot top: hot chocolate

Hounds on an island: frankfurters and beans

Houseboat: banana split

Hug one: glass of orange juice

Ice on rice: rice pudding with
ice cream

Life preservers: doughnuts

Lighthouse: bottle of ketchup

L. T.: Lettuce and tomato sandwich

Mama on a raft: marmalade on toast

Mats: pancakes

Mike and Ike: salt and
pepper shakers

Million on a platter: plate of
baked beans

Mississippi mud: mustard

Nervous pudding: jello

Oh gee: Orange juice

One from the Alps: Swiss
cheese sandwich

Pink stick: strawberry ice cream

Popeye: spinach

Put a hat on it: add ice cream

Put out the lights and cry: order of
liver and onions

Rabbit food: lettuce

Raft: slice of toast

Shake one in the hay: strawberry
milkshake

Shivering Eve: apple jelly

Sneeze: pepper

Splash of red noise: bowl of
tomato soup

Splash out of the garden: bowl of
vegetable soup

Sun kiss: orange juice

Sweep the kitchen: plate of hash

Throw it in the mud: add
chocolate syrup

Twist it, choke it, and make it
cackle: chocolate malted
milkshake with egg

Vermont: maple syrup

Wart: olive

Wax: American cheese

Wimpy: hamburger

Wrecked hen fruit: scrambled eggs

Yellow paint: mustard

Yum-yum: sugar

Diner Talk

NOTES ON THE MUSIC

The following are brief tributes to the artists who composed and/or originally performed the songs that were recorded especially for this Menus and Music volume by the Bay City All Stars, a group of top San Francisco musicians.

Shake Rattle and Roll
Charles Calhoun
Hill & Range Songs

Big Joe Turner, born in 1911 in Kansas City, Missouri, was one of rock & roll's forefathers. He started his career as a singing bartender in Kansas City in the late 1920s and made his debut recording of "Roll 'em Pete" with boogie-woogie pianist Pete Johnson. In 1938, Turner and Johnson took part in John Hammond's now legendary "From Spirituals to Swing" concert at Carnegie Hall, which helped spark the boogie-woogie craze of the late 1930s and early 1940s. In 1951, while playing New York's Apollo Theater with Count Basie, Turner was heard by Atlantic co-owner Ahmet Ertegun, who signed him to the label. Between 1951 and 1956, he had fourteen top ten rhythm & blues hits for the company, including "Shake Rattle and Roll" in 1954. Bill Haley's cover version of the song became one of the nation's ten best-selling records later that year. Other Joe Turner hits include "Chains of Love," "Sweet Sixteen," "Corrina, Corrina," and "Rock a While." Turner had been singing for over twenty years when he recorded these songs in the 1950s, his extraordinary, powerful voice providing a link between the blues and rock & roll. Joe Turner died in 1985. He was inducted into the Rock & Roll Hall of Fame in 1987.

My Guy
William Smokey Robinson
Jobete Music Co., Inc.

Mary Wells, born in 1943 in Detroit, Michigan, was offered a recording contract by Berry Gordy with his newly formed Motown (short for Motor Town) Records. Gordy entrusted Wells's career to Smokey Robinson, who composed a series of irresistible melodies for her and provided understated pop arrangements to back her smooth vocal style. She became the label's first glamorous star. In 1964, "My Guy" was number one in the United States and in the top five in Great Britain. Mary Wells opened for the Beatles in 1964 at their request. Her other hits include "You Beat Me to the Punch" and "Two Lovers." She also recorded duets with Marvin Gaye, including "What's the Matter with You Baby" and "Once Upon a Time." She left Motown at the height of her success, but none of her subsequent releases with other labels were as successful as her Motown recordings.

Mustang Sally
Bonny Rice
Fourteenth Hour Music, Inc.
Springtime Music, Inc.

Wilson Pickett, born in 1941 in Prattville, Alabama, was raised in Detroit, where he sang with several local rhythm & blues groups. In 1964, Jerry Wexler signed him to Atlantic Records and brought him to Memphis, where he recorded with Booker T and the MGs. At his best, Pickett's swaggering singing style, full of shouting, jubilant cries, and powerful screams, is galvanizing. "Mustang Sally" was his cover of a tune first recorded by Mack Rice. He scored seventeen top ten rhythm & blues hits between 1964 and 1972, including "In the Midnight Hour," "Land of 1,000 Dances," and "Funky Broadway." Pickett was the esteemed role model in the award-winning soul music film *The Commitments,* and he was inducted into the Rock & Roll Hall of Fame in 1991.

Heat Wave
Eddie Holland, Lamont Dozier, Brian Holland
Stone Agate Music

"Heat Wave" put Martha and the Vandellas on the charts and made them one of Motown's most successful recording groups in the early 1960s. Martha Reeves, born in 1941 in Alabama, was trained in both classical and gospel music. She joined the Motown organization in 1961, working as a secretary.

She also supervised Little Stevie Wonder during office hours and did occasional backing vocals on recording sessions. When Berry Gordy offered her a chance to record for the label, she put together a trio with Annette Beard and Rosalind Ashford, and in 1962 she led the group on their debut release under the name Martha and the Vandellas. "Heat Wave" was a major hit in 1963, and from then on the group had a string of hits including "Dancing in the Streets," "Jimmy Mack," "I'm Ready for Love," and "Nowhere to Run." They were inducted into the Rock & Roll Hall of Fame in 1995.

My Girl
William Smokey Robinson, Ronald White
Jobete Music Co., Inc.

The Temptations, founded by former members of two Detroit vocal groups and fronted by two lead singers, Eddie Kendricks and David Ruffin, was signed to Motown Records in 1961 by Berry Gordy. Gordy gave the group their name and teamed them with songwriter-producer Smokey Robinson. In 1964, "The Way You Do the Things You Do" became their first major hit and reached number eleven on the pop chart. "My Girl" was the group's first number-one song in 1965. Their trademark choreography, vocal harmonies, and great lead singers made them Motown stars. During the late 1960s and early 1970s, their hits included "It's Growing," "Since I Lost My Baby," and "Get Ready." The Temptations were inducted into the Rock & Roll Hall of Fame in 1989.

Searchin'
Jerry Leiber, Mike Stoller
Anne-Rachel Music
Jerry Leiber Music
Mike Stoller Music

Between 1956 and 1961, the Coasters, a Southern California vocal quartet, cut a nearly unbroken string of nationwide hits, all written and produced by Jerry Leiber and Mike Stoller. Leiber and Stoller's finely crafted and often comical musical vignettes captured the rebellious spirit of teenage America.

Notes on the Music

They introduced string arrangements to rhythm & blues records and married rhythm & blues to the pop tradition. Originated as the Robins, the Coasters were America's most popular black rock & roll group by the end of the 1950s. "Searchin'," number three on the pop charts and the number one rhythm & blues song in 1957, was the first of the group's four gold records. Other hit singles include "Yakety Yak," "Charlie Brown," and "Poison Ivy." The Coasters were inducted into the Rock & Roll Hall of Fame in 1987, the same year as songwriters/producers Leiber and Stoller.

Johnny B. Goode
Chuck Berry
Isalee Music Company

Rock and Roll Music
Chuck Berry
Isalee Music Company

Songwriter, guitar player, and lyricist Chuck Berry, born Charles Edward Anderson Berry in 1926 in St. Louis, has influenced nearly every rock musician. His playing turned the guitar into a lead instrument, and after him rock performers would find it impossible to achieve major status without taking a hand in the creation of their own music. Berry's lyrics captured the teenage experience and widened the gap between music that glorified youth and more adult-oriented rhythm & blues and pop. His clean diction made his songs almost like poetry with rock guitar accompaniment. In 1955, while in Chicago, Berry met Muddy Waters, who advised him to approach the Chess Label. Chess gave him a recording contract, and "Maybellene" became Berry's debut single. Between 1955 and 1960, he had seventeen rhythm & blues top twenty entries, including "Rock and Roll Music" in 1957 and "Johnny B. Goode" in 1958. Both the Beatles and the Rolling Stones acknowledge their debt to Chuck Berry. In 1959 he was arrested for violation of the Mann Act and sent to prison until 1964. He continued writing hits such as "No Particular Place to Go," "You Never Can Tell," and "Reelin' and Rockin'" after his release from prison until 1979, when he was imprisoned for tax evasion.

Notes on the Music

Berry wrote *Chuck Berry: The Autobiography* and was the subject of the documentary film *Hail! Hail! Rock 'n' Roll*. He was inducted into the Rock & Roll Hall of Fame in 1986.

Blueberry Hill
Al Lewis, Vincent Rose, Larry Stock
Chappell & Co.
Sovereign Music Company

Singer, pianist, and songwriter Fats Domino, born Antoine Domino in 1929 in New Orleans, became America's second-best-selling rock artist in the late 1950s, outsold only by Elvis Presley. His rolling boogie-style piano playing, the infectious charm of his Cajun-inflected tenor voice, and his good nature made him a popular rocker. By featuring saxophone solos in his songs, he made that instrument an integral part of early rock & roll. In 1956, "Blueberry Hill," a tune from a 1941 Gene Autry movie, was number two on the pop chart and a number-one rhythm & blues hit. Other hits include "Ain't That a Shame," "I'm Walkin'," "Whole Lot of Lovin'," and "I'm Ready." Fats Domino was inducted into the Rock & Roll Hall of Fame in 1986.

Please Mr. Postman
Holland, Gorman, Dobbins, Garrett, Bateman
Jobete Music Co., Inc.
Stone Agate Music

Berry Gordy signed five suburban Detroit teenagers, Gladys Horton, Katherine Anderson, Juanita Cowart, Georgeanna Tillman, and Wanda Young, to his Motown Record label and gave them the name the Marvelettes. They were the first artists to give his fledgling label a number-one hit with "Please Mr. Postman" in 1961. (The Beatles covered the song in 1963.) Although the Marvelettes never had a chart-topper again, they continued recording such hits as "Don't Mess with Bill" and "Playboy" until disbanding in the early 1970s.

Green Onions

Booker T. Jones, Stephen Cropper, Al Jackson, Lewis Steinberg
Irving Music, Inc.

Booker T and the MGs (which stands for either Memphis Group or the sports car) was the primary house rhythm section behind many of the hits released by Stax Records in Memphis. Formed in 1962, the group's first big hit was "Green Onions," which evolved from a blues riff they had improvised while waiting to record an advertising jingle. The quartet is heard on Wilson Pickett's "In the Midnight Hour," Sam and Dave's "Hold on I'm Comin'," and "Walkin' the Dog" by Rufus Thomas. "Green Onions" was reissued in the late 1970s in the U.K. and became a top ten hit there in 1979. Booker T. Jones became a successful producer for Bill Wither's "Ain't No Sunshine" and Willie Nelson's album *Stardust,* and was inducted into the Rock & Roll Hall of Fame in 1992. The group reunited to play in the rhythm section of Bob Dylan's all-star thirtieth anniversary concert celebration, and in 1993 they toured as Neil Young's backup band.

But It's Alright

Jerome Jackson, Pierre Tubbs
Famous Music Corp.
Pamelarosa Music Inc.

J. J. Jackson's "But It's Alright" was a nationwide hit in 1966. Before that, Jackson, a singer, songwriter, and organist, had worked as an arranger for Jack McDuff and Jimmy Witherspoon in New York. He left for England in 1966 and recorded "But It's Alright" with British studio musicians. Jackson was never again to match the success of that recording. He later moved to Los Angeles, where he worked as a disc jockey, and he also had a cameo performance in the film *Car Wash,* which has been sampled by rappers.

Notes on the Music

Where Did Our Love Go?
Eddie Holland, Lamont Dozier, Brian Holland
Stone Agate Music

The Supremes were the most commercially successful female group of the 1960s and the decade's third best-selling popular group, following the Beatles and Elvis Presley. Diana Ross, Mary Wilson, and Florence Ballard epitomized the Motown sound and the label's sophisticated style. The group was formed when the girls were still in high school. In 1961, Berry Gordy signed them to Motown, where they had only moderate success until song-writers/producers Holland-Dozier-Holland hit on the right formula to show-case Diana Ross's distinctive vocal style. "Where Did Our Love Go" was the country's best-selling record and The Supremes' first number-one hit in 1964, selling over two million copies. Other hits include "Baby Love," "Come See About Me," "Stop! In the Name of Love," "Back in My Arms Again," "I Hear a Symphony," "You Can't Hurry Love," and "You Keep Me Hangin' On." Diana Ross left the Supremes in 1969 and became a star of Las Vegas, television, and the movies, including *Lady Sings the Blues, Mahogany,* and *The Wiz*. The Supremes were inducted into the Rock & Roll Hall of Fame in 1988.

Shop Around
Berry Gordy, Jr., William Smokey Robinson
Jobete Music Co., Inc.

Ooo Baby Baby
William Smokey Robinson, Warren Moore
Jobete Music Co., Inc.

The Miracles—the most successful rhythm & blues group formed in Detroit in the mid-1950s—were founded by Smokey Robinson while he was still in high school. They became the Miracles in 1958, when they made their initial recording with producer Berry Gordy at the newly formed Motown Records. The Miracles recorded "Shop Around" in 1960, giving Motown its first major U.S. hit. The beautiful ballad "Ooo Baby Baby" rose to number sixteen on the pop chart and was the number-four rhythm & blues song in 1965. The Miracles had twenty-seven top forty hits, including "You Really Got

Notes on the Music

a Hold on Me" (covered by the Beatles in 1963), "Going to a Go-Go," "The Tears of a Clown," "I Second That Emotion," and the elegant "The Tracks of My Tears." Smokey Robinson sang lead in his silky, romantic falsetto on almost all of the group's recordings. Recognized as a great singer and as one of the premier writers of love songs in pop music, he was inducted into the Rock & Roll Hall of Fame in 1987.

Tutti Frutti

Richard Penniman, Dorothy LaBostrie
EMI Blackwood Music under license from ATV Music

Little Richard, born Richard Penniman in 1935 in Macon, Georgia, was one of the first black artists to cross over to the national white pop charts, and he did it with no holds barred. A flamboyant performer with a flair for wild hair-dos and makeup, his frenetic singing style of joyous whooping, wild falsetto, and ecstatic screams elicited hysteria in his audiences. His "Tutti Frutti," origi-nally an obscene ditty that was given new words by Dorothy LaBostrie, was recorded in 1955 in the New Orleans studio used by Fats Domino. The song's nonsense syllables simulated instrumental sounds in the tradition of scat singers from Louis Armstrong on. "Tutti Frutti" rose to number seventeen in the United States and sold to both black and white fans. The shrieks and propulsive beat of hits like "Long Tall Sally" (the first record by a black artist to outsell its white cover by Pat Boone), "Good Golly Miss Molly," and "Lucille" epitomize the wild, rebellious nature of rock & roll. Paul McCartney, for one, idolized Little Richard's singing.

Little Richard quit show business in the late 1950s to become a minister. He went to England in 1962 to sing gospel music, but ended up singing "Long Tall Sally" in order to compete with Sam Cooke, who was on the same bill; his performance drove the audience into a frenzy and Little Richard back to rock & roll. Since then he has appeared in the movie *Down and Out in Beverly Hills,* become a fixture on television talk shows, and made occasional record-ings, including the best-selling 1992 *Shake It All About* for Disney. Little Richard is near the top of any list of rock & roll pioneers and was inducted into the Rock & Roll Hall of Fame in 1986.

You Send Me

Sam Cooke
ABKCO Music, Inc.

Sam Cooke, born in 1931 in Clarksdale, Mississippi, the son of a Baptist minister, grew up in Chicago. A superb singer, he first performed publicly with his brother and two sisters in their church quartet and later sang lead in the gospel group the Soul Stirrers during the first half of the 1950s. When Cooke recorded his debut pop album, he used a pseudonym in order to avoid offending his gospel fans. Found out, he was forced to leave the quartet and so began his career in secular music. In 1957, he recorded "You Send Me," and it became a number-one hit. His other top forty hits include "Wonderful World," "Chain Gang," "Twistin' the Night Away," "Bring It on Home to Me," "Little Red Rooster," and "Shake." In 1960 he was signed by RCA, for whom he recorded a string of influential self-composed pop music hits until 1963, when he was fatally shot in a Los Angeles motel room. Just seven years after recording "You Send Me," Sam Cooke had eighteen top twenty hits to his name. His tunes have been covered by such diverse artists as Otis Redding, Al Green, Cat Stevens, the Animals, Rod Stewart, and the Rolling Stones. He was inducted into the Rock & Roll Hall of Fame in 1986.

Notes on the Music

A-1 Diner

Gardiner, Maine

Perched on eighteen-foot-high stilts above the Cobbosseecontee River, so that its entryway is level with the bridge it abuts, the A-1 is one of only two classic Worcester diners remaining in Maine. Structurally unchanged since 1946, it still contains its original mahogany booths, marble counter, blue and black tilework, and scalloped stainless-steel back wall. In fact, proprietors Neil Andersen and Michael Giberson (who took the diner over from Giberson's father in 1988), have removed many of the "modernizations" made over the years, so their diner's true personality could reemerge. The A-1 offers vegetarian entrées and creative new dishes like Vietnamese Bouillabaisse, Mushroom Pasticcio, and Tuscan Black-Backed Sole with Oriental Greens, alongside such diner staples as cheeseburgers, macaroni and cheese, and meat loaf.

A-1 Diner

Venison and Root Vegetable Stew

Rutamousse

Pumpkin-Pecan Whoopie Pies

Venison and Root Vegetable Stew

2 cups chicken stock (page 228) or canned low-salt chicken broth
3 cups dry red wine
½ cup molasses
½ cup balsamic vinegar
½ cup plus 4 tablespoons olive oil
1 garlic clove, minced
1 teaspoon kosher salt
2 teaspoons dried thyme
2 teaspoons ground pepper
10 juniper berries, ground
4 pounds venison, trimmed of fat and cut into 1-inch chunks
2 onions, coarsely chopped
¼ cup all-purpose flour
6 carrots, peeled and cut into 1-inch slices
6 parsnips, peeled and cut into 1-inch slices
6 turnips or 2 small rutabagas, peeled and cut into 1-inch cubes

In a large bowl, combine the stock or broth, wine, molasses, vinegar, ½ cup of the olive oil, garlic, salt, thyme, pepper, and juniper berries. Add the venison and mix well. Cover with plastic wrap and marinate for 1 to 2 hours at room temperature. Drain the marinade and reserve it.

In a Dutch oven or large, heavy pot over medium heat, heat 2 tablespoons of the remaining olive oil and brown the venison on all sides in batches. Remove each batch of venison and set aside on a plate; continue until all the meat is browned. Heat the remaining 2 tablespoons olive oil over medium heat and sauté the onions until golden, about 7 minutes. Return the venison to the pot, stir in the flour, and cook for 3 to 4 minutes.

Stir in the marinade, increase heat to high, and bring the liquid to a boil. Reduce heat to low and simmer the stew for 30 minutes. Add the carrots, parsnips, and turnips or rutabagas and cook 30 minutes more, or until the vegetables are tender. Taste and adjust the seasoning, if necessary. Serve warm.

Makes 8 servings

Rutamousse

1 large rutabaga, peeled and cut into 1-inch cubes
4 potatoes, peeled and cut into 1-inch cubes
3 tablespoons butter
¼ cup light cream or half-and-half
Salt and freshly ground pepper to taste

In a large pot of salted boiling water, cook the rutabaga and potatoes for 15 minutes, or until the vegetables are tender; drain.

Using an electric mixer, beat the rutabagas and potatoes until smooth. Or, mash them with a potato masher or force through a ricer. Pour into a warm bowl and stir in the butter, cream or half-and-half, salt, and pepper. Serve immediately.

Makes 4 servings

Pumpkin-Pecan Whoopie Pies

Whoopie pies were originally small cakes made from leftover cake batter for Pennsylvania Dutch children. The name may derive from the whoop of joy the children made on receiving such a treat.

2½ cups all-purpose flour
1 teaspoon ground cinnamon
2 teaspoons ground ginger
½ teaspoon ground mace
1 teaspoon salt
1 teaspoon baking powder
1 teaspoon baking soda
1 cup (2 sticks) butter at room temperature
2 cups packed brown sugar
3 large egg yolks
2 cups canned pumpkin
¾ cup finely chopped pecans

Filling
¾ cup (1½ sticks) butter at room temperature
3 cups powdered sugar, sifted
2 teaspoons vanilla extract
1 egg white
Pinch *each* ground cinnamon, ginger, and mace

   Preheat the oven to 350°F. Grease 2 baking sheets. In a small bowl, stir together the flour, cinnamon, ginger, mace, salt, baking powder, and baking soda.

   In the bowl of an electric mixer, cream the butter and brown sugar together. Add the egg yolks one at a time and mix well after each addition. Stir in the pumpkin and pecans and mix well. Add the flour mixture and stir just until combined; do not overmix.

A-1 Diner

Drop the batter by heaping tablespoonfuls onto the baking sheets, leaving 3 inches between each one. When the baking sheets are full, smack them on a table or counter to flatten the batter slightly. Bake in the preheated oven for 11 to 12 minutes, or until the cookies are lightly browned. Let cool completely on a wire rack.

To make the filling: In the bowl of an electric mixer, cream the butter until fluffy and pale. Add the powdered sugar and mix until incorporated. Mix in the remaining ingredients and beat until smooth.

Spread the filling on half of the cookies; top each with another cookie.

Makes 12 to 15 whoopie pies

American City Diner

Washington, D.C.

American City is Jeffrey Gildenhorn's built-from-scratch-by-Kullman reproduction of the classic freestanding diner, complete with a monitor roof, jukeboxes at every booth, a 1949 Coca-Cola machine that dispenses 6½-ounce Cokes, Necco Wafers, and Bazooka Bubble Gum at the cash register, and a large neon clock with the simple admonition: EAT. Overlooking the exterior is a copy of a vintage billboard featuring Mom, Dad, Buddy, Sis, and Pooch, all smiling out of the family car under the caption, "There's no way like the American Way." Inside, the red, white, and blue menus tell customers that "Uncle Sam wants you to try Dana's homemade pies, puddings & cakes!" American City's huge popularity indicates that customers respond well to a menu featuring Stuffed Bell Peppers with Tomato Sauce, Yankee Pot Roast, and Chicken Fried Steak, listening to the Wurlitzer jukebox, and what Gildenhorn calls "a period of Americana which represents strong family ties—the time of outdoor barbecues and a wholesome, happy, uncomplicated life."

American City Diner

Hungarian Goulash

Chicken Pot Pie

Sweet and Sour Stuffed Cabbage

Cathedral Window Dessert

Hungarian Goulash

As with most slowly braised dishes, this goulash will taste best if it is allowed to cool, then is refrigerated overnight and reheated before serving. Serve with buttered noodles.

3 tablespoons vegetable oil
1½ cups chopped onion
1 green bell pepper, cored, seeded, and finely diced
1 large garlic clove, minced
2 pounds beef stew meat, cut into ¾-inch cubes
6 cups water
4 teaspoons salt
¼ teaspoon cayenne pepper
1½ pounds (about 3 large) potatoes, peeled and diced
One 16-ounce can chopped tomatoes with juice

In a Dutch oven or large heavy pot over low heat, heat the vegetable oil and sauté the onion, green pepper, and garlic until tender and lightly browned, about 10 minutes. Add the stew meat and sauté until browned on all sides. Stir in the water, salt, and cayenne. Increase the heat to high and bring the liquid to a boil. Reduce heat to low, cover, and simmer the goulash for 1½ hours, or until the meat is tender.

Add the potatoes, cover the pan, and cook for 15 minutes, or until the potatoes are tender. Stir the tomatoes and juice into the goulash and cook 5 to 7 minutes longer.

Makes 6 servings

American City Diner

Chicken Pot Pie

Pastry

1 cup all-purpose flour

½ teaspoon salt

⅓ cup vegetable shortening

2 tablespoons cold water

Filling

6 tablespoons vegetable oil or rendered chicken fat (page 233)

1 onion, diced

1 potato, peeled and diced

½ cup thinly sliced carrot

2 tablespoons unbleached all-purpose flour

½ teaspoon salt

½ teaspoon ground pepper

2½ cups chicken stock (page 228) or canned low-salt chicken broth

2 cups diced cooked chicken meat

½ cup fresh or frozen peas

2 tablespoons finely chopped pimientos (optional)

To make the pastry: Stir the flour and salt together in a medium bowl. Cut in the vegetable shortening with a pastry cutter or 2 knives until the shortening pieces are the size of peas. Sprinkle with the water and stir with a fork to form a mass. Or, process the flour, salt, and shortening in a food processor until the shortening pieces are the size of peas. Add the water and process until the mixture forms a mass. Shape the dough into a disk, cover with plastic wrap, and chill in the refrigerator for at least 30 minutes.

Preheat the oven to 400°F. To make the filling: In a medium saucepan over medium heat, heat the vegetable oil or chicken fat and sauté the onion, potato, and carrot until tender, about 10 minutes. Stir in the flour, salt, and pepper. Gradually add the chicken stock or broth, stirring constantly to make a thick sauce. Add the diced chicken meat, peas, and pimientos, if using. Set aside and keep warm.

Remove the dough from the refrigerator and cut into 5 equal pieces. On a lightly floured surface, roll out each piece of dough into a circle large enough to cover an individual ovenproof crock. Divide the filling equally among 6 crocks. Top each crock with a circle of pastry. Pierce the crusts several times near the center with a fork and place the crocks on a baking sheet. Bake in the preheated oven for 30 minutes, or until the crusts are golden brown.

Makes 6 pot pies

Sweet and Sour Stuffed Cabbage

1 green cabbage (about 4 pounds)
1 pound lean ground beef
1 large egg, beaten
Salt and freshly ground pepper to taste
Juice of 1 lemon
1 white onion, chopped
2 tablespoons long-grain white rice
6 tomatoes, peeled, seeded, and chopped (page 232)
One 8-ounce can tomato sauce
1 cup golden raisins
1½ tablespoons sugar
1 teaspoon dried oregano
1 teaspoon sweet Hungarian paprika

Separate 12 large cabbage leaves from the cabbage. Cut out the tough bottom part and reserve the leaves. Core the cabbage and cut the cabbage into 1-inch dice.

Bring a large pot of water to a boil and cook the reserved cabbage leaves for 5 minutes, or until tender. Using a slotted spoon, transfer the leaves to a colander and cool them under cold running water. Pat the leaves dry with paper towels and place the leaves flat on a cutting board.

In a large bowl, mix together the ground beef, egg, salt, pepper, half the lemon juice, 2 tablespoons of the chopped onion, and the rice. Spoon 1½ tablespoons of the meat mixture into the center of a leaf, fold the bottom of the leaf up to cover the filling, and fold in the sides. Roll the leaf into a cylinder. Repeat with the remaining leaves and filling.

In a large pot or saucepan, combine the remaining onion and the chopped cabbage. Place the cabbage rolls on top of the onion and cabbage. Pour in the tomatoes, tomato sauce, raisins, remaining lemon juice, sugar, oregano, and paprika. Season with salt and pepper. Cover the pot and cook over low heat for about 2 hours, or until the rice is tender and the sauce is thickened.

Makes 6 servings

Cathedral Window Dessert

The mixed colors of the fruit cocktail in this gelatin dessert give it its name.

3 envelopes plain gelatin
1 cup boiling water
One 14-ounce can sweetened condensed milk
2 cups heavy (whipping) cream
One 8-ounce can fruit cocktail

In a small bowl, combine the gelatin and boiling water; stir to dissolve the gelatin and let cool.

In a medium bowl, stir together the condensed milk and cream. Stir in the gelatin mixture and fruit cocktail. Chill in the refrigerator for at least 3 hours before serving.

Makes 6 servings

Bette's Oceanview Diner

Berkeley, California

Bette's was started by Bette Kroening, her husband Manfred, and her friend Sue Conley fifteen years ago, when "a California diner was an oxymoron." But Bette and Sue had grown up on the East Coast and wanted to create a neighborhood restaurant patterned after those they had known and loved. The result is Bette's, a stylish nouveau diner with excellent food, snappy and cheerful service, and a casual no-hassle atmosphere. The combination of old-fashioned portions with new-fashioned cooking skill and attention to detail make Bette's well-loved in Berkeley: on weekends people often wait up to two hours to be seated. The menu offers soufflé pancakes, huevos rancheros, scrapple, crab cakes, homemade soups, and corned beef hash. The diner itself features black and white tile, deep red upholstered booths, and a vintage '57 Seeburg jukebox with more than five thousand 45s. (Bette says she bought the jukebox "even before we bought the stove!")

Bette's Oceanview Diner

Strawberry Soufflé Pancake

Corned Beef Hash with Poached Eggs

Phil's Salmon Hash

Lemon Bars

Strawberry Soufflé Pancake

A signature dish at Bette's, this quick, puffy pancake starts on the stove top and is finished under the broiler.

3 eggs, separated
½ cup half-and-half
¼ cup all-purpose flour
½ teaspoon granulated sugar
Pinch of salt
1½ tablespoons butter, melted
1 tablespoon Grand Marnier
1 cup sliced fresh strawberries mixed with 1 tablespoon granulated sugar
Vegetable oil for cooking
Sifted powdered sugar for dusting

Preheat the broiler. In a medium bowl, beat 2 of the egg yolks with the half-and-half until well mixed. (Reserve the third yolk for another purpose.) Gradually stir in the flour until just combined. Add the sugar, salt, butter, and Grand Marnier and mix until well blended.

In a large bowl, beat the egg whites until soft peaks form. Fold the egg whites into the batter and gently stir in most of the strawberries; reserve a few to place on top of the pancake just before it goes under the broiler.

Heat an 8-inch, ovenproof, nonstick frying pan or seasoned cast-iron skillet over medium-high heat. Film the pan with oil. Pour the batter into the pan, reduce heat to medium, and cook until the bottom of the pancake is browned and bubbles appear around the edges, 5 to 8 minutes.

Place the reserved strawberries evenly on top of the batter and place the pan 4 to 5 inches below the preheated broiler. Cook until the top of the pancake is browned and the center is just set but still soft. Gently slide the pancake onto a warm serving plate, dust with powdered sugar, and serve immediately.

Makes 1 serving

Corned Beef Hash with Poached Eggs

Rich and delicious, this hash has a crisp golden crust with a creamy center. It is best served with poached fresh eggs and toasted rye bread. The hash may be made the day before serving and refrigerated until just before serving time.

3 large russet potatoes, peeled and cut into ½-inch dice (6 cups)
3 cups diced cooked corned beef brisket
4 garlic cloves, minced
1 tablespoon red wine vinegar
¾ cup heavy (whipping) cream
Freshly ground pepper to taste
Poached Eggs (recipe follows)

In a large pot of boiling salted water, cook the potatoes until tender, 5 to 10 minutes; drain.

In a large bowl, combine the potatoes, corned beef, garlic, vinegar, and cream and stir until thoroughly combined.

In a large sauté pan or skillet, cook the hash over medium heat, stirring frequently, until the cream bubbles and reduces by half. Season the hash with pepper and let it cool completely.

On a griddle or in a lightly oiled skillet over medium heat, fry the hash for 5 minutes on each side, or until a crust forms. Cut the hash into wedges, top with poached eggs, and serve immediately.

Makes 8 servings

Poached Eggs

The fresher the eggs, the better they poach and the better they taste.

1 tablespoon vinegar
Pinch of salt
4 eggs

In a medium sauté pan or skillet, combine the vinegar and salt with water to a depth of 2 inches. Bring to a boil, then reduce heat to a low simmer. Crack the eggs one at a time onto a saucer and slide each into the water. Cook 2 minutes for soft yolks and 3 minutes for firmer yolks. Using a slotted spoon, carefully remove the eggs in the order in which they were added.

Makes 2 servings

Phil's Salmon Hash

This is delicious served with steamed fresh asparagus.

Court Bouillon
1 onion
2 celery stalks
6 fresh parsley sprigs
Chopped green onion tops to taste
1 cup dry white wine
3 quarts water
1½ teaspoons salt

2 pounds salmon fillets
½ cup (1 stick) butter at room temperature
1 onion, finely diced
3 unpeeled russet potatoes, cut into ¾-inch dice
Leaves from ¼ bunch fresh dill, snipped
Salt and freshly ground pepper to taste
Clarified butter for frying (page 230)
Lemon wedges and fresh dill sprigs for garnish

To make the court bouillon: In a large stockpot or saucepan, combine the onion, celery, parsley, green onion tops, wine, and water. Bring to a boil over high heat, reduce heat to a simmer, and cook for 30 minutes. Remove from heat and stir in the salt.

Remove the skin and bones from the salmon fillets and cut them into 4-ounce pieces. To a large sauté pan or skillet, add enough court bouillon to just cover the fish. Bring the liquid to a gentle simmer over medium heat. Add the salmon and poach for 3 to 4 minutes, or until the salmon is opaque on the outside but translucent in the center. Using a slotted spoon, carefully remove the salmon and let cool.

In a medium sauté pan or skillet, melt 1 to 2 tablespoons of the butter over medium heat. Add the onion and a little water and cook until the onion is tender but not brown; remove from heat and let cool.

In a large pot of boiling salted water, cook the diced potatoes until tender, about 10 minutes. Drain the potatoes well. Mash some of the potatoes, keeping the rest whole.

In a large bowl, combine the salmon, potatoes, onion, dill, remaining butter, salt, and pepper; use your fingers to break the salmon apart. Mix to blend. Form the mixture into 8 patties and refrigerate for 1 hour.

In a large sauté pan or skillet, heat 1 tablespoon clarified butter over medium heat and sauté the salmon patties, in batches if necessary, until golden brown, 3 to 4 minutes on each side. Repeat the process if necessary to cook any remaining patties. Place the patties on 8 warm plates, garnish with lemon wedges and dill sprigs, and serve immediately.

Makes 8 servings

Lemon Bars

Crust

½ cup (1 stick) plus 1 tablespoon cold butter

⅜ cup packed brown sugar

1½ cups all-purpose flour

½ teaspoon salt

Lemon Filling

5 eggs

1 cup plus 2 tablespoons granulated sugar

⅓ cup all-purpose flour

¾ teaspoon baking powder

¼ teaspoon salt

1 tablespoon grated lemon zest

½ cup fresh lemon juice

Sifted powdered sugar for sprinkling

To make the crust: Preheat the oven to 350°F. Combine all the crust ingredients in a food processor and process until small crumbs form. Or, to make by hand, combine the brown sugar, flour, and salt in a medium bowl. Using a pastry cutter or 2 knives, cut in the butter until small crumbs form. Press the mixture into the bottom of a 9-by-13-inch baking pan and bake in the preheated oven for 15 minutes, or until set. Let cool while making the filling.

To make the filling: In a large bowl, combine the eggs and sugar and beat for 3 to 5 minutes, or until very pale and thick. Sift the flour, baking powder, and salt together and fold into the egg mixture. Add the lemon zest and lemon juice and fold in until blended. Immediately pour the filling onto the crust, spread evenly, and bake in the preheated oven for 20 minutes, or until lightly browned. Let cool to room temperature in the pan. Using a knife that has been dipped in hot water, cut into 12 bars. To serve, sprinkle the lemon bars with powdered sugar.

Makes 12 bars

Boogie's Diner

Aspen, Colorado

Boogie's Diner was built in 1987 by Boogie Weinglass, who wanted a comfortable, friendly place to serve excellent food. The ambience of the upstairs diner is complete with great jukebox hits, stainless steel and Formica, and an atrium and outdoor patio. The menu features a large selection of vegetarian dishes, fresh fish, and gourmet salads and soups; Boogie's was the first restaurant in Aspen to feature the American Heart Association's "Dine to Heart's Delight." The popular diner serves seven hundred to eight hundred meals a day, and everything is made from scratch. Traditional housemade desserts include chocolate cake, Dutch apple pie, and chocolate cream pie, as well as the Buttermilk Pie that follows. Boogie's was awarded the International Food Manufacturer's Association award for culinary excellence in 1994.

Boogie's Diner

Thai Chicken Peanut Soup

Smoked Chicken and Wild Rice Salad

Buttermilk Pie

Thai Chicken Peanut Soup

1 tablespoon peanut or other vegetable oil

1 cup finely chopped onion

1 *each* red, yellow, and green bell pepper, cored, seeded, and finely diced

2 leeks, minced (white part only)

3 shallots, minced

2 garlic cloves, minced

6 cups can crushed tomatoes with juice

8 cups chicken stock (page 228) or canned low-salt chicken broth

One 6-ounce can peeled green chilies

½ bunch fresh cilantro, stemmed and minced

½ teaspoon red pepper flakes

1 teaspoon ground pepper

6 cups cooked black beans

2 cups cooked chicken meat, cut into 1-inch cubes

¾ cup creamy peanut butter

1 tablespoon mint jelly

½ cup roasted peanuts

In a soup pot over medium heat, heat the oil and sauté the onion, bell peppers, leeks, shallots, and garlic until the onion is translucent, about 5 minutes. Stir in the tomatoes, tomato juice, stock or broth, green chilies, cilantro, pepper flakes, and black pepper. Reduce heat to low and simmer for 15 minutes. Stir in the beans, chicken, peanut butter, and mint jelly; raise heat to high and bring to a boil. Ladle 1 cup of soup into each bowl, sprinkle with peanuts, and serve immediately.

Makes 12 servings

Smoked Chicken and Wild Rice Salad

1 cup wood chips

4 large chicken breast halves

1 cup wild rice

3 cups water

1 teaspoon salt

1 tablespoon olive oil

½ tablespoon white wine vinegar

Salt and freshly ground pepper to taste

½ bunch green onions, including some green tops, chopped

1 head lettuce

Curried Yogurt-Chutney Dressing (recipe follows)

1 *each* red and yellow bell pepper, cored, seeded, and cut into julienne

1 banana, sliced (optional)

Light a fire in a charcoal grill. Soak the wood chips in warm water to cover for 30 minutes. When the coals are medium-hot, drain the wood chips and sprinkle them over the coals. Grill the chicken for 5 minutes on each side, then cover the grill and cook for 5 minutes on each side, or until browned and springy to the touch. Transfer to a cutting board to cool. Cut the chicken into thin slices. Remove and discard the skin and bones.

To make the wild rice: Rinse the rice. In a medium saucepan, combine the water and salt and bring to a boil. Add the rice, reduce heat to low, cover, and cook for 40 minutes, or until the water is absorbed. Transfer the rice to a medium bowl. Stir in the olive oil, vinegar, salt, and pepper and toss to combine. Let cool, then stir in the green onions.

Arrange whole lettuce leaves on 4 chilled plates. Place a mound of torn lettuce in the center of each plate and top with ¼ cup wild rice and some sliced chicken. Spoon some curried yogurt-chutney dressing over. The salads with red and yellow peppers, and sliced banana, if desired.

Makes 4 servings

Curried Yogurt-Chutney Dressing

This dressing may be made 1 day before serving.

1 garlic clove, minced
1½ tablespoons white wine vinegar
2 tablespoons fresh lemon juice
¾ tablespoon curry powder
½ cup Major Grey's chutney
Salt and freshly ground pepper to taste
⅓ cup olive oil
½ cup nonfat plain yogurt
1½ tablespoons water
¼ cup minced fresh cilantro

In a blender or food processor, combine the garlic, vinegar, lemon juice, curry powder, chutney, salt, and pepper and blend until smooth. With the machine running, add the olive oil in a thin stream until emulsified. Transfer the dressing to a bowl and stir in the yogurt, water, and cilantro. Cover and refrigerate for up to 1 day.

Makes about 1½ cups

Buttermilk Pie

½ cup (1 stick) butter, melted

1 cup sugar

3 eggs

1 tablespoon cornstarch

1 teaspoon vanilla extract

½ cup buttermilk

1 unbaked 8-inch pie shell (page 232)

Preheat the oven to 450°F. In a medium bowl, mix the butter and sugar together. Beat in the eggs one at a time. Add the cornstarch, vanilla, and buttermilk and beat until thoroughly combined. Pour the filling into the prepared pie shell.

Place the pie in the preheated oven and immediately reduce the heat to 350°F. Bake for 45 minutes, or until a knife inserted near the center comes out clean. Serve the pie warm or chilled.

Makes one 8-inch pie

Bubba's Diner

San Anselmo, California

Noted San Francisco Bay Area chef Steve Simmons, former executive chef under Bradley Ogden at Lark Creek Inn and One Market, cooks up both old- and new-fashioned American diner food at Bubba's. An honest-to-goodness 1950s-style diner with chrome-plated stools at the counter and red Naugahyde booths, Bubba's features such homey diner fare as buttery biscuits, house-made pickles, and blue plate specials including Fried Chicken, Liver and Onions, and Pot Roast. Simmons uses his talents to give the traditional food a refined edge, and on his menu customers will find a Portobello Mushroom Sandwich side by side with Homemade Meat Loaf with BBQ Sauce, and Tofu and Grilled Vegetable Scramble right under Mashed Potato Pancake with Fried Egg. Simmons and his wife, Beth, foster small-town community spirit at Bubba's with such events as the monthly Theme Night, when customers dress for a Hawaiian luau or other such party, and kids' parties like Easter Basket Day and Gingerbread Day.

Bubba's Diner

Counter Pickles

Fried Chicken

Pot Roast

Baked Meat Loaf

Fruit Cobbler

Banana-Butterscotch Pie

Counter Pickles

Large crocks of these pickles line the counter at Bubba's. A variation of bread and butter pickles, they are a great snack to have in the refrigerator.

25 pickling cucumbers, preferably Kirbys, cut into ¼-inch-thick slices
½ cup kosher salt
5 cups white wine vinegar
5 cups sugar
2 tablespoons mustard seed
2 bay leaves

One day before pickling: In a large bowl, toss the cucumber slices and salt together until all the slices are lightly coated. Cover with ice cubes and let stand overnight.

The next day, combine the remaining ingredients in a large nonaluminum saucepan and bring to a boil. Remove the cucumber slices from the salt and water and rinse under running water. Place the cucumbers in hot sterilized pint jars, leaving ¼ inch headspace, and pour in the hot pickling brine to completely cover the cucumbers. Seal according to the manufacturer's directions. Refrigerate the pickles for 24 hours before using.

Fried Chicken

½ cup kosher salt
½ teaspoon dried sage
¼ teaspoon dried thyme
2 fryer chickens, cut into 12 pieces, or 6 chicken breast halves
     and 6 chicken thighs
2 cups buttermilk

1½ to 2 cups all-purpose flour
1 tablespoon salt
2 teaspoons ground pepper
1 teaspoon cayenne pepper
Peanut oil for frying

The day before frying, mix the salt, sage, and thyme together in a plastic bag. Add the chicken pieces and toss until they are evenly and lightly coated; refrigerate for 30 minutes. Rinse the chicken under running water, place in a shallow dish, and pour the buttermilk over. Cover the dish with plastic wrap and refrigerate overnight.

The next day, combine the flour, salt, pepper, and cayenne in another shallow dish. Drain the buttermilk from the chicken pieces, but do not dry them. Dredge the chicken in the flour mixture.

Heat a large, heavy skillet or sauté pan over high heat. Add 1 inch of peanut oil, and heat until almost smoking. Carefully place the chicken in the hot oil, leaving plenty of space between the pieces. Reduce the heat to medium and cook the chicken for 8 to 10 minutes on each side, or until golden brown. Drain the chicken on wire racks with paper towels underneath.

Makes 6 servings

Pot Roast

This is delicious served with mashed potatoes or spaetzle.

4 tablespoons peanut oil
2 to 3 pounds chuck roast, tied with string
2 onions, chopped
2 carrots, peeled and chopped
2 celery stalks, chopped

3 garlic cloves, chopped

2 cups dry red wine

6 tomatoes, chopped

4 fresh thyme sprigs

4 cups chicken stock (page 228) or canned low-salt chicken broth, heated

Salt and freshly ground pepper to taste

Preheat the oven to 400°F. In a large, heavy skillet over high heat, heat 2 tablespoons of the peanut oil and brown the chuck roast evenly on both sides. Transfer the roast to a Dutch oven or a roasting pan.

In the same skillet over low heat, heat the remaining 2 tablespoons peanut oil and cook the onions, carrots, celery, and garlic, stirring frequently, for 20 to 30 minutes, or until the vegetables are tender and browned. Transfer the vegetables to the pan with the meat. Add the red wine to the skillet, stir to scrape up the browned bits from the bottom of the pan, and pour the liquid into the pan with the meat.

Add the tomatoes and thyme to the pan and pour in the hot chicken stock or broth. Cover with a lid or aluminum foil and bake in the preheated oven for 2 hours, or until tender.

Remove the roast from the pan and cover it loosely with aluminum foil. Using a slotted spoon, transfer the vegetables to a blender or food processor and purée. Stir the purée back into the liquid in the baking pan. Place the pan over medium heat, season the mixture with salt and pepper, and cook for 10 minutes. Strain the sauce through a sieve. Taste and adjust the seasoning, if necessary. Remove the strings from the roast, slice the meat thinly, and arrange it on each plate. Ladle some sauce over and serve immediately.

Makes 4 to 6 servings

Meat Loaf

Serve with a generous helping of mashed potatoes.

Sauce
2⅔ cups ketchup
1⅓ cups Dijon mustard
6 tablespoons packed brown sugar

1 tablespoon vegetable oil
1 onion, diced
6 garlic cloves, minced
4 pounds lean ground beef
1 cup oatmeal
4 eggs, beaten
2 cups chopped spinach
Salt and ground pepper to taste
8 bacon slices

To make the sauce: In a medium bowl, stir together all the ingredients until thoroughly combined. Set aside.

Preheat the oven to 400°F. In a small sauté pan or skillet over medium heat, heat the oil and sauté the onions until translucent, about 5 minutes. Stir in the garlic and sauté 2 minutes. Transfer to a small bowl and set aside to cool.

In a large bowl, combine the onion mixture, ground beef, oats, eggs, spinach, salt, pepper, and 2 cups of the sauce until well blended. Pat the meat mixture into a 9-by-5-inch loaf pan and arrange the bacon slices on the top. Cover the meat loaf with the remaining sauce. Cover the loaf pan with aluminum foil and bake in the preheated oven for 45 minutes, or until browned and firm. Let cool for 10 to 15 minutes before slicing.

Makes 8 servings

Fruit Cobbler

This old-fashioned dish is delicious for both dessert and breakfast.

Topping
2 cups all-purpose flour

¾ cup sugar

4 teaspoons baking powder

½ teaspoon salt

¼ cup vegetable shortening

1 egg

¾ cup milk

Filling
6 cups fresh berries or sliced fruit

1 cup sugar, or to taste

2 tablespoons all-purpose flour

Preheat the oven to 425°F. Butter a 9-by-13-inch baking dish. To make the topping: In a large bowl, mix the flour, sugar, baking powder, and salt together until thoroughly combined. Cut in the vegetable shortening with a pastry cutter or 2 knives until the mixture is the texture of coarse meal. Add the egg and milk and stir with a fork until just combined.

To make the filling: In a large bowl, combine all the ingredients. Pour into the prepared dish or casserole and spoon the dough over evenly. Bake in the preheated oven 35 to 45 minutes, or until golden brown.

Makes 6 to 8 servings

Banana Butterscotch Pie

This pie makes an ideal companion for piping hot cups of coffee.

Oat Crust
½ cup packed brown sugar

¼ cup vegetable shortening

½ teaspoon baking soda

¾ cup all-purpose flour

¾ cup rolled oats

Filling
1 cup packed brown sugar

¼ teaspoon salt

5 tablespoons all-purpose flour

1 tablespoon cornstarch

2 cups milk, scalded

3 egg yolks

3 tablespoons butter

1 teaspoon vanilla extract

3 ripe bananas, sliced

Topping
1 cup heavy (whipping) cream

1 tablespoon powdered sugar, sifted

1 teaspoon vanilla extract

To make the oat crust: In a medium bowl, combine all the ingredients and mix until well blended. Empty into a 9-inch pie plate and pat and press the mixture evenly around the bottom and sides of the plate. Bake the crust in the preheated oven for 8 to 10 minutes, or until lightly browned.

To make the filling: In a medium, heavy saucepan, combine the sugar, salt, flour, and cornstarch. Gradually stir in the milk and cook over medium heat, stirring constantly, until thick and smooth; continue cooking for 15 minutes, stirring occasionally.

In a small bowl, beat the egg yolks until pale. Whisk ¼ cup of the hot milk mixture into the yolks; pour this mixture back into the saucepan. Cook, stirring constantly, for 2 to 3 minutes, or until very thick. Remove from heat and stir in the butter and vanilla; let cool.

Layer the banana slices over the bottom of the prepared pie crust and pour in the filling; spread to even the top. Let cool completely.

Just before serving, make the topping: In a small, deep bowl, whip the cream, powdered sugar, and vanilla together until soft peaks form. Top the pie with the topping and serve immediately.

Makes one 9-inch pie

Buckhead Diner

Atlanta, Georgia

This sophisticated diner offers a unique gourmet dining experience in a comfortable yet ritzy ambience. A custom creation that was opened in 1987, the Buckhead inspires a feeling of nostalgic warmth while evoking a contemporary sense of luxury. Reminiscent of an Orient Express railcar, it has an exterior of polished stainless steel, an imported Italian marble floor, granite countertops, booths of exotic hardwoods and rich fabrics, and muted one-of-a-kind light fixtures.

The modern American cuisine at the Buckhead highlights original snacks, grilled specialties, fresh seafood, signature sandwiches, and fun desserts, along with classic diner foods. A few of the popular dishes include Crispy Salt and Pepper Calamari, Celery Mashed Potatoes, and White Chocolate Banana Cream Pie, the James Beard Foundation's choice for Best Dessert in the country in 1994. The diner is known as the place in Atlanta to "view the stars" and regularly attracts such celebrities as Bernadette Peters, Elton John, Luther Vandross, Arnold Schwarzenegger, Nicole Kidman, Robert Goulet, and the Indigo Girls.

Buckhead Diner

Lump Crab Cakes

Roast Marinated Leg of Lamb with
Root-Vegetable Mash and Ratatouille Sauce

Bourbon Pecan Pie

Lump Crab Cakes

1 pound fresh jumbo lump crabmeat

½ cup freshly chopped green onions, including some green tops

¼ cup diced roasted red peppers (page 234)

⅓ cup mayonnaise

1 tablespoon Worcestershire sauce

¼ teaspoon dry mustard

½ teaspoon curry powder

1 tablespoon Old Bay seasoning

3 slices white bread, diced

¼ cup extra-virgin olive oil

1 tablespoon vinegar

Salt and freshly ground pepper to taste

4 handfuls (4 ounces) baby field greens such as mâche, arugula,
	mizuna, Bibb, and romaine

2 tablespoons peanut oil

Pick through the crabmeat to remove any shells, being careful not to break the lumps. In a medium bowl, combine the crabmeat, green onions, and peppers and stir gently to mix.

In a small bowl, combine the mayonnaise, Worcestershire sauce, mustard, curry powder, Old Bay seasoning, and bread and stir until well mixed. Add the mayonnaise mixture to the crab and gently mix together.

In a medium bowl, combine the olive oil, vinegar, salt, and pepper and whisk together to make a vinaigrette. Toss the greens with the vinaigrette.

In a large sauté pan or skillet over medium heat, heat the peanut oil. Scoop out ½-cup portions of the crab mixture and form into cakes. Cook the crab cakes for about 3 minutes per side, or until golden brown, adding more oil as needed. Arrange the salad on 4 plates, top with the crab cakes, and serve immediately.

Makes 4 servings

Roast Marinated Leg of Lamb

Marinade
4 garlic cloves
Leaves from 2 fresh basil sprigs
Leaves from 2 fresh rosemary sprigs
1 bunch fresh parsley, stemmed
1 pinch red pepper flakes
2 cups olive oil

2½ pounds lamb top round
Salt and freshly ground pepper to taste
Root-Vegetable Mash (recipe follows)
Ratatouille Sauce (recipe follows)

To make the marinade: In a blender, combine the garlic, basil, rosemary, parsley, and pepper flakes, and purée. With the machine running, gradually add the olive oil to make a smooth sauce. Place the lamb in a nonaluminum baking pan. Pour the marinade over the lamb, cover, and refrigerate for 4 to 5 hours.

Remove the meat from the refrigerator 30 minutes before cooking. Preheat the oven to 350°F. Remove the meat from the marinade and season it with salt and pepper. Heat a large skillet over high heat, add the meat, and brown it on both sides. Place the meat in a roasting pan and bake in the preheated oven for 20 to 30 minutes, or until an instant-read thermometer inserted in the lamb registers 120°F for medium. Place a mound of root-vegetable mash on each of 4 warm plates, top with the lamb, and serve with ratatouille sauce.

Makes 4 servings

Root-Vegetable Mash

2 tablespoons vegetable oil
1 onion, chopped
2 garlic cloves, minced
1 celery root, cut into ¼-inch dice
2 carrots, peeled and cut into ¼-inch dice
2 parsnips, peeled and cut into ¼-inch dice
2 turnips, peeled and cut into ¼-inch dice
1 cup chicken stock (page 228) or canned low-salt chicken broth
2 pounds potatoes, peeled and cut into pieces
2 cups milk
½ cup (1 stick) butter
Salt and freshly ground pepper to taste

In a large saucepan over low heat, heat the vegetable oil and cook the onion until translucent, about 3 minutes. Stir in the garlic and sauté for 1 minute. Add the celery root, carrots, parsnips, and turnips and cook for 3 to 4 minutes. Stir in the chicken stock or broth and cook until the vegetables are tender, about 10 minutes.

In a large pot of salted boiling water, cook the potatoes until tender, about 15 minutes. Drain well. Add the potatoes to the pan of root vegetables.

In a small saucepan, combine the milk and butter. Bring to a boil over medium heat. Using a hand mixer, purée the root vegetables and potatoes. Gradually stir in the hot milk mixture until a creamy, but not soupy, consistency is reached. Season with salt and pepper and serve immediately.

Makes 4 servings

Ratatouille Sauce

2 tablespoons olive oil
1 onion, cut into ¼-inch dice
1 garlic clove, minced

1 *each* red and yellow bell pepper, cored, seeded, and cut into ¼-inch dice
¼ teaspoon dried oregano
¼ teaspoon red pepper flakes
1 zucchini, cut into ¼-inch dice
1 yellow squash, cut into ¼-inch dice
1 eggplant, cut into ¼-inch dice
1 cup chicken stock (page 228) or canned low-salt chicken broth
1½ cups tomato juice
½ teaspoon salt
½ teaspoon ground white pepper

In a large sauté pan or skillet over low heat, heat the olive oil and cook the onion until tender, about 5 minutes. Stir in the garlic and cook 1 minute more. Stir in the red and yellow peppers and cook for 1 minute. Add the oregano, red pepper flakes, zucchini, yellow squash, and eggplant and cook 1 minute more. Raise heat to high, add the chicken stock or broth and tomato juice, and bring to a boil. Reduce heat to low and simmer for about 2 minutes. Add the salt and pepper. Serve hot or at room temperature.

Makes about 8 cups

Bourbon Pecan Pie

A perennial favorite at the Buckhead Diner, this pie is delicious served with whipped cream or ice cream.

4 cups cake flour
⅔ cup granulated sugar
1¼ cups (2½ sticks) cold butter, cut into pieces
1 egg, lightly beaten
1½ cups plus 2 tablespoons packed brown sugar
½ cup (1 stick) butter, melted

¼ cup corn syrup

¼ maple syrup

4 eggs

¼ cup bourbon whiskey

3 cups (1 pound) pecans

In a medium bowl, combine the flour and sugar, and stir until thoroughly combined. Using a pastry cutter or 2 knives, cut in the butter until the mixture resembles coarse crumbs. Stir in the egg until the dough forms a mass. Form into a flattened disk. Cover with plastic wrap and refrigerate for at least 30 minutes.

Preheat the oven to 350°F. On a lightly floured surface, roll the pastry dough out to a thickness of ⅛ inch. Fit the dough into a 10-inch pie pan. Trim and crimp the edges.

In a medium bowl, combine the brown sugar, melted butter, corn syrup, maple syrup, eggs, and bourbon whiskey and mix until thoroughly combined. Pour the nuts into the crust, then pour the filling over. Bake in the preheated oven for about 30 minutes, or until the crust is golden brown and the filling is firm. Let cool completely. Cut into wedges to serve.

Makes one 10-inch pie; serves 8

Camp Washington Chili

Cincinnati, Ohio

At the same location, run by the same owners, and with the same fixtures—stainless-steel counter, checkered floor, neon signs, jukeboxes at every booth—since 1940, Camp Washington Chili is dedicated to serving its famous chili twenty-four hours a day. The hospitable waitresses serve travelers from across the country, as well as locals who sometimes get a craving for the chili at midnight. (Great breakfasts and double-decker sandwiches are also served any time of the day.) The chili is so renowned that it's been featured on both "CBS Morning News" and MTV; the diner's been visited by famous musicians such as Lonnie Mack, Jimmy Buffet, and the Eagles; and the mayor of Cincinnati declared June 12 Camp Washington Chili Day! Although the recipe is a family secret, the exact spices of which are known only to proprietors John Johnson and his wife, Antigone, they have graciously provided Menus and Music with a delicious, similar version of their Cincinnati-style chili. (Note: For those of you outside the Cincinnati area, the five ingredients that make chili "five-way" are spaghetti noodles, kidney beans, chili, diced onions, and Cheddar cheese—see recipe on page 76.)

Camp Washington Chili

Cincinnati-Style Greek-American Chili

Cincinnati-Style Greek-American Chili

Begin this recipe 2 days before you plan to serve the chili. Soak the kidney beans overnight and prepare the chili the day before serving; refrigerate it overnight for a better marriage of flavors.

Beans
1 pound (2 cups) dried red kidney beans
One 4-ounce chunk salt pork
1 cup dry red wine
1 garlic clove, minced
1 teaspoon dried dill
½ teaspoon dried oregano
½ teaspoon dried summer savory
1 onion, stuck with 2 whole cloves

Chili
2 tablespoons powdered pure chili, or more to taste
¼ teaspoon ground cinnamon
¼ teaspoon ground cloves
1 teaspoon cumin seed
¼ teaspoon ground ginger
½ teaspoon dry mustard
⅛ teaspoon freshly grated nutmeg
1 teaspoon dried oregano, crumbled
2 tablespoons olive oil
3 yellow onions, minced
1 tablespoon minced garlic
1 cup chopped green bell pepper
2 teaspoons coarse salt
2 pounds coarsely ground lean beef, preferably top round
Two 38-ounce cans whole Italian tomatoes, with juice
2 beef bouillon cubes

To make the beans: Rinse and pick through the beans to remove any stones. Add the beans to a large pot of boiling water and boil for 2 minutes. Remove from heat and let soak overnight.

The next day, blanch the salt pork in simmering water for 10 minutes; drain. Add the wine to the beans and enough water to cover the beans by 2 inches. Place the pot over medium-low heat and bring to a simmer. Gently stir in the garlic, dill, oregano, and savory. Bury the onion and salt pork in the center of the beans. Cover and gently simmer for 1½ to 2 hours, or until tender. Set aside.

To make the chili: Using a mortar and pestle or spice grinder, grind the powdered chili, cinnamon, cloves, cumin seed, ginger, mustard, nutmeg, and oregano together; set aside.

In a large, heavy pot over medium-high heat, heat the olive oil until it begins to sizzle. Stir in the onions and garlic and sauté for 5 minutes, or until the onion turns golden. Stir in the green pepper, salt, and ground spice mixture and sauté 2 minutes longer. Add the ground beef and stir to break up any clumps. Cook for 3 minutes, or until the beef is no longer pink. Add the tomatoes and their juice; crush the tomatoes while stirring them in. Bring the chili back to a simmer.

Transfer 2 cups of the bean broth to a small saucepan and bring it to a boil. Dissolve the bouillon cubes in the liquid and return it to the chili pot. Taste and adjust the seasoning as necessary. Simmer the chili at least 2 and preferably 4 hours, adding more water as necessary. Remove the pot from heat and let cool; cover and refrigerate the chili overnight. The next day, reheat the chili and serve.

Makes 6 servings

Five-Way Chili

Arrange a bed of spaghetti on a plate and spoon the beans over. Cover the spaghetti and beans with chili and sprinkle some diced onion over. Top with a handful of shredded Wisconsin Cheddar cheese.

Cheese Coney

Start with a warm hot dog bun and a wiener. Add a dab of mustard and fill the hot dog with chili until it almost overflows. Sprinkle some diced onion on top of the chili and top the whole thing off with shredded Wisconsin Cheddar cheese.

Camp Washington Chili

Clarksville Diner

Decorah, Iowa

In areas of the country where they're not common, diners are often established by transplanted easterners who grew up with them. Such is the case with the Clarksville Diner, originally of Clarksville, New Jersey (where it was known as Swifty's). Gordon Tindall missed this diner of his youth when he moved to Iowa, so in 1988 he acquired it just before its slated demolition. He moved it halfway across the country, then spent the next four years doing careful restoration, which involved locating salvaged parts from other diners. The Clarksville Diner finally opened in Decorah in 1992, even though the right side was nearly demolished by an automobile just a few weeks before the scheduled opening, causing Tindall to postpone the opening to make major repairs. In 1994, Tindall succeeded in getting his diner listed on the National Register of Historic Places. The Clarksville Diner serves traditional diner food only—breakfast any time, meat loaf every day, and daily specials like liver and onions. The cooks make everything from scratch, so the dishes vary depending on what's fresh in the kitchen that day.

Clarksville Diner

Nick's Greek Platter

Gordon's Chili with Quesadillas

Cheryl's Peach and Blueberry Pie

Nick's Greek Platter

This is owner Gordon Tindall's favorite breakfast dish, but he says his customers order it all day long. Gordon and his son Ian created the recipe as a tribute to all the people of Greek ancestry in the diner industry (which is why they call it "Nick's"), and they serve it on a platter with a Greek design.

1 tablespoon vegetable oil

1 red potato, sliced

½ green bell pepper, cored, seeded, and chopped

2 eggs

2 Kalamata olives, pitted and chopped

¼ cup crumbled feta cheese

¼ cup chopped fresh spinach leaves

1 tablespoon butter at room temperature

1 pita bread

Satzeki Sauce (recipe follows)

1 tomato, chopped

Freshly ground pepper to taste

In a medium sauté pan or skillet over medium heat, heat the vegetable oil and cook the potato and bell pepper, stirring frequently, until browned, about 15 minutes; set aside and keep warm in a 200°F oven. In a medium bowl, beat the eggs and stir in the olives, feta cheese, and spinach until well blended. Spread the butter on both sides of the pita bread, put the bread on a baking sheet, and place in the oven.

Heat a 7-inch omelette pan over medium-high heat and add oil to coat the bottom. Pour the egg mixture into the hot omelette pan, then reduce heat to medium. Cook for 15 seconds, or until the edges begin to sizzle a little, then give the pan a shake. (If the pan isn't hot enough, the eggs will stick.) Cook until lightly browned on the bottom. Using a metal spatula, turn the omelette over and cook until lightly browned on the second side; remove from heat.

To serve, place the pita bread on a warm plate. Place the omelette on top of the pita bread with the best-looking side up. Place a dollop of satzeki sauce in the center and top with the tomato and a sprinkle of pepper. Spoon the bell pepper mixture alongside and serve at once.

Makes 1 serving

Satzeki Sauce

You can vary the ingredient amounts to make this sauce to your taste. Gordon Tindall doesn't measure any of the ingredients—he just puts in what he thinks is right.

¼ cup plain yogurt
¼ cup sour cream
¼ teaspoon celery salt
Pinch of salt
½ tablespoon fresh lemon juice
1 minced garlic clove or to taste
¼ teaspoon dried oregano
Pinch of ground pepper
1 cucumber, peeled, seeded, and finely chopped

In a medium bowl, combine all the ingredients and stir until well blended.

Makes about 1 cup

Gordon's Chili with Quesadillas

Gordon takes pride in not using hamburger, kidney beans, or macaroni in his chili. And he makes it hot. As he says, "Those wanting 'church chili' can get it at church suppers!"

1½ pounds (3 cups) dried pinto beans

About 8 cups chicken stock (page 228) or canned low-salt chicken broth

Beef concentrate to taste

2 celery stalks, finely chopped

2 carrots, peeled and diced (optional)

1 onion, finely chopped

1 green bell pepper, cored, seeded, and chopped

8 pickled jalapeño chilies, minced

4 garlic cloves, minced

Salt and freshly ground pepper to taste

1 cup all-purpose flour for dredging

1 tablespoon ground cumin, plus more for sprinkling

1 tablespoon chili powder, plus more to taste

2 pounds beef bottom round, cut into ½-inch cubes

One 48-ounce can tomatoes, chopped

Quesadillas (recipe follows)

Rinse and pick through the beans and discard any stones. Put the beans in a large bowl of cold water to cover and soak overnight. (They will triple in size.)

The next day, drain and rinse the beans. Put them in a large pot and add chicken stock or broth to cover the beans by 2 inches. (The chili will be a little soupy when done.) Add the beef concentrate, celery, optional carrots, onion, bell pepper, jalapeños, garlic, salt, and pepper. Bring the liquid to a boil over medium heat, then reduce heat to low and let simmer.

In a shallow bowl, combine the flour, 1 tablespoon cumin, and 1 table-spoon chili powder and stir until well mixed; dredge the beef in the flour mixture. Lightly coat a large sauté pan or skillet with vegetable oil and heat over high heat. Brown the meat on all sides. Add the meat to the pot of simmering beans. Add more chili powder and cumin to taste and simmer for 45 minutes. Add the chopped tomatoes and more chili powder to taste. Simmer for 45 minutes more, stirring occasionally. Spoon the chili into bowls and sprinkle with cumin seed. Serve hot, with quesadillas.

Makes 8 servings

Clarksville Diner

Quesadillas

A quesadilla is like a grilled cheese sandwich made with tortillas instead of bread.

8 flour tortillas
2 cups (8 ounces) grated Monterey jack cheese

Preheat the oven to 200°F. Heat a dry skillet over medium heat and add 1 tortilla. Sprinkle ¼ cup cheese over the tortilla and heat until the cheese melts. Fold the tortilla in half and put on a plate in the warm oven. Repeat to cook the remaining quesadillas. Serve immediately.

Makes 8 quesadillas

Cheryl's Peach and Blueberry Pie

Crust
⅓ cup vegetable shortening
1 cup all-purpose flour
½ teaspoon salt
3 tablespoons cold water

Filling
3 pounds fresh peaches, peeled, pitted, and sliced,
    or 6 cups frozen sliced peaches
½ cup sugar
1 teaspoon ground cinnamon
¼ cup all-purpose flour
½ cup fresh or frozen blueberries

Topping
¾ cup all-purpose flour

½ cup sugar

6 tablespoons cold butter

Preheat the oven to 400°F. To make the crust: With a pastry cutter or 2 knives, cut the vegetable shortening into the flour and salt until the mixture is the texture of coarse meal. Sprinkle in the water and mix with a fork, then press together in a ball. Or, process the shortening, flour, and salt in a food processor to the texture of coarse meal. Add the water and process until the mixture forms a mass. Form the dough into a flattened disk. Cover and refrigerate for at least 30 minutes. Roll the dough out on a lightly floured board to a thickness of ⅟₁₆ inch. Fit the dough into a 9-inch pie plate, trim the edges, and crimp.

To make the filling: In a medium bowl, combine the peaches, sugar, cinnamon, and flour and stir until well blended. Pour the mixture into the pie shell and sprinkle the blueberries on top.

To make the topping: In a small bowl, combine the flour and sugar. With a pastry cutter or 2 knives, cut the butter into the flour and sugar until it is crumbly. Sprinkle the topping over the pie. Bake in the preheated oven for 1 hour and 15 minutes, or until the topping is golden brown.

Makes one 9-inch pie

The Corvette Diner

San Diego, California

A fun and energetic place for people in San Diego to enjoy comfort food while slurping sodas and listening to jukebox hits, the award-winning Corvette Diner features blue plate specials, a soda fountain, and a deejay spinning records from his booth. Favorite dishes include Chicken Parmesan, Spaghetti, Meatball Sandwiches, and the Footlong Chili-Chez Dog Deluxe, as well as such south-of-the-border inspirations as Dante's Inferno Hamburger with jalapeños and Baja Fish Tacos. The Corvette's menu trumpets "Simple Food for Complex Times" and proclaims "Life is uncertain . . . Eat dessert first." If you do, you can choose from their many shakes, floats, smoothies, sundaes, cakes, and pies, which include The World's Smallest Brownie Chocolate Sundae, the 14-Carrot Cake, and the Peppermint Twist. A favorite with children, the Corvette Diner is also a founding member of the National Corvette Museum.

The Corvette Diner

Harvest Soup

"Hot Rod" Chopped Salad

Corvette Diner Meat Loaf

Crème Brûlée

Harvest Soup

This soup is best made the day before serving so the flavors have a chance to ripen.

1 butternut squash, peeled, seeded, and cut into 2-inch cubes
1 tablespoon olive oil
1 whole garlic head
4 tablespoons butter
2 onions, diced
2 tablespoons all-purpose flour
6 cups chicken stock (page 228) or canned low-salt chicken broth, heated
1 cup heavy (whipping) cream
Salt and freshly ground white pepper to taste
½ bunch fresh chives, snipped

Preheat the oven to 400°F. Rub the butternut squash cubes with the olive oil and arrange them in a single layer in a baking dish. Wrap the garlic head in aluminum foil and place in the preheated oven on a separate shelf from the squash. Bake for 30 to 45 minutes, or until the squash is tender and lightly browned and the garlic is soft. Set aside to cool.

In a soup pot or large saucepan, melt the butter over medium heat and sauté the onions until translucent, about 5 minutes. Stir in the flour and cook, stirring constantly, for 5 minutes. Gradually whisk in the chicken stock or broth. Reduce heat to low. Cut about ¼ inch off the pointed end of the garlic head and squeeze out the roasted garlic. Add the squash and garlic purée to the soup and simmer for 1 hour. Remove from heat and let cool slightly.

Transfer the soup to a blender or food processor and purée, in batches if necessary. Return to the pan. Stir in the cream, salt, and pepper and heat the soup to a simmer over low heat. Ladle into soup bowls, garnish with the chives, and serve.

Makes 6 to 8 servings

"Hot Rod" Chopped Salad

2 heads iceberg or romaine lettuce, thinly sliced
¾ cup chopped, pitted Kalamata olives
1 grilled chicken breast half, chopped
½ cup chopped pepperoni
3 Roma tomatoes, peeled, seeded, and chopped (page 232)
½ cup shredded fresh basil
1 cup (4 ounces) grated mozzarella cheese
1 cup Dijon Vinaigrette (recipe follows), or to taste
1 red bell pepper, cored, seeded, and cut into matchsticks for garnish

In a large bowl, toss together all the ingredients except the red pepper. Garnish the salad with the red pepper and serve.

Makes 4 to 6 servings

Dijon Vinaigrette

1 egg yolk
3 tablespoons Dijon mustard
½ tablespoon honey
½ cup red wine vinegar
1½ tablespoons Worcestershire sauce
¼ teaspoon salt
½ teaspoon ground pepper
1½ cups olive oil

In a blender or food processor, blend the egg yolk, mustard, honey, vinegar, Worcestershire sauce, salt, and pepper together. With the machine running, gradually pour in the olive oil in a thin, steady stream until emulsified.

Makes about 2 cups

Corvette Diner Meat Loaf

2 pounds lean ground beef
½ cup ketchup
2 tablespoons A-1 steak sauce
¾ cup shredded carrot
¾ cup diced onion
¾ cup minced fresh parsley
1 teaspoon ground pepper
¾ teaspoon celery salt
¾ teaspoon dry mustard
¼ teaspoon garlic powder
1¼ cups quick-cooking oats
2½ teaspoons prepared horseradish
2 jumbo eggs, beaten
½ cup tomato sauce
2 tablespoons clover honey
Mashed potatoes (page 231)
Brown gravy (page 227)

Preheat the oven to 375°F. Coat a 9-by-5-inch loaf pan with vegetable oil.

In a large bowl, mix the ground beef, ketchup, steak sauce, carrot, onion, parsley, pepper, celery salt, mustard, garlic powder, oats, horseradish, and eggs together just until combined. Pat the meat mixture into the prepared loaf pan. Using the tines of a fork, criss-cross the top of the loaf decoratively. Bake in the preheated oven for 45 minutes, or until browned and firm to the touch. Remove the meat loaf from the oven.

In a small bowl, stir together the tomato sauce and honey. Cover the meat loaf with the tomato mixture. Return the meat loaf to the oven and bake for 15 minutes.

Let the meat loaf cool for 20 minutes before slicing. Serve with mashed potatoes and brown gravy.

Make 6 servings

Crème Brûlée

A crisp caramelized sugar coating contrasts wonderfully with the creamy custard underneath. The custard can be made 1 to 3 days ahead, but it should be caramelized just before serving.

3 cups heavy (whipping) cream
½ cup milk
6 egg yolks
¾ cup sugar
1 tablespoon vanilla extract
¾ cup packed brown sugar

Preheat the oven to 350°F. In a small, heavy saucepan, combine the cream and milk. Heat over low heat until bubbles form around the edges of the pan.

In a medium bowl, combine the egg yolks, sugar, and vanilla and whisk until they are slightly thickened and pale. Whisk in ½ cup of the hot cream mixture. Return this mixture to the pan and whisk to blend. Strain the custard through a fine-meshed sieve. Divide the custard evenly among six 6-ounce custard cups or ramekins.

Set the cups or ramekins in a baking dish and pour water into the dish to halfway up the sides of the cups. Bake in the preheated oven for 25 to 30 minutes, or until the custards are set but quiver slightly when shaken.

To finish, preheat the broiler. Push 2 tablespoons of the brown sugar through a small sieve with the back of a spoon to evenly cover each custard. Place the custards under the broiler, very close to the heat, until the sugar melts and caramelizes, 1 to 2 minutes (be careful not to let it burn). Let cool for a few minutes and serve.

Makes 6 custards

Country Club Restaurant and Pastry Shop

Philadelphia, Pennsylvania

Owned and operated by Noel and Simone Perloff, the Country Club is a 250-seat, ten-thousand-square-foot Fodero-constructed diner that was built in 1968 from twenty individual diner cars. Replacing and named after an original 1956 restaurant, it is still pure diner, from the tile flooring to the counter and grill to the booths lining the walls of the first two dining rooms. The Country Club is renowned in Philadelphia for its award-winning home-style cooking, particularly its oven-fresh desserts and its Jewish-American and European dinner specialties, many of which were handed down through generations of the Perloff family. Along with meat loaf, chicken croquettes, and club sandwiches, the menu includes Chicken Soup with Matzo Balls, Sweet Noodle Kugel, Whitefish Salad, and delicious cherry and blueberry blintzes. In 1996, the Country Club celebrated its fortieth birthday and welcomed its *20 millionth* customer.

J. CORERIS

Country Club Restaurant and Pastry Shop

Chicken Soup with Matzo Balls

Roast Brisket of Beef with Kasha Varnishkas

Bread Pudding

Chicken Soup with Matzo Balls

1 whole chicken with giblets (about 3 pounds)

1 carrot, peeled and sliced

1 celery stalk, sliced

1 red onion, quartered

1 ounce parsley root, trimmed, scraped, and cut into 1-inch pieces

¼ teaspoon minced fresh dill

Pinch of salt

¼ teaspoon ground pepper

8 cups water

Matzo Balls

4 eggs, separated

1 cup matzo meal (available in Jewish delicatessens and some grocery stores)

¼ cup vegetable oil

¼ teaspoon salt

Pinch of ground pepper

Place the chicken and its giblets in a large soup pot. Add the vegetables, dill, salt, pepper, and water; bring to a boil. Reduce heat to low and simmer for 2 hours, skimming any foam that rises to the surface. Remove the chicken from the pot and set aside to cool. Shred the meat from the bones and return the meat to the soup pot. Let the soup cool and skim off any fat that rises to the surface.

To make the matzo balls: In a large bowl, beat the egg whites until stiff peaks form. In a medium bowl, mix the egg yolks and all the remaining ingredients. Gently fold the egg whites into the matzo meal mixture. Cover and refrigerate for at least 1 hour.

Form the matzo mixture into 2-tablespoon-sized balls (do not handle too much). Bring the chicken soup to a boil and drop in the matzo balls. Reduce the heat to low, cover, and simmer for 20 minutes. Serve with bow-tie pasta or egg noodles.

Makes 6 servings

Roast Brisket of Beef with Kasha Varnishkas

1 garlic clove, minced

1 teaspoon salt

1 teaspoon ground pepper

3 pounds beef brisket

1 onion, quartered

1 carrot, peeled and sliced

1 celery stalk, diced

4 cups water

Kasha Varnishkas (recipe follows)

Preheat the oven to 350°F. Combine the garlic, salt, and pepper and rub the brisket on all sides with this mixture. Transfer the meat to a Dutch oven or large, heavy ovenproof casserole and bake in the preheated oven, uncovered, until the meat is browned. Remove from the oven and add the onion, carrot, celery, and water. Reduce the heat to 325°F and bake, uncovered, for 4½ hours, or until very tender. Remove from the oven and let the brisket cool slightly. Trim off any fat and slice the meat against the grain. Arrange the meat on a large platter and surround with the vegetables. Serve with kasha varnishkas.

Makes 6 servings

Kasha Varnishkas

Kasha, or roasted buckwheat, has a nuttier flavor than buckwheat groats.

1 cup medium kasha

2 eggs, beaten

2 cups chicken stock (page 228) or canned low-salt chicken broth

½ cup vegetable oil, rendered chicken fat (page 233), or butter

½ onion, diced

1 teaspoon minced garlic

4 green onions, white part only, thinly sliced
1 cup cooked bow-tie pasta
1½ teaspoons kosher salt
¼ teaspoon ground pepper
¼ bunch fresh dill, snipped

Preheat the oven to 350°F. In a medium bowl, mix together the kasha and egg until each grain is coated with egg. In a small sauté pan or skillet over medium-high heat, sauté the kasha mixture, stirring constantly, until the kasha grains separate and are lightly toasted.

In a medium saucepan, bring the chicken stock or broth to a boil; stir in the kasha. Remove the pan from heat and pour the mixture into a baking dish. Cover the dish with aluminum foil and bake in the preheated oven for 10 minutes. Remove from the oven and fluff the kasha mixture with a spoon. Cover again and bake 15 minutes longer.

Meanwhile, in a medium sauté pan or skillet over medium heat, heat the oil, chicken fat, or butter and sauté the diced onion until translucent, about 5 minutes. Add the garlic and green onions and sauté for 2 minutes.

In a large bowl, combine the kasha mixture, onion mixture, pasta, salt, pepper, and dill. Serve warm.

Makes about 4 cups

Bread Pudding

1½ cups heavy (whipping) cream

1½ cups half-and-half

½ cup (1 stick) butter

2 eggs at room temperature

½ cup sugar

¼ teaspoon vanilla extract

½ teaspoon ground cinnamon

⅛ teaspoon orange extract

1½ cups cubed challah bread or other egg bread

½ cup golden raisins

2 apples, peeled, cored, and diced

¼ cup orange juice or water

¾ cup walnuts, chopped

½ cup packed brown sugar

Preheat the oven to 300°F. In a large saucepan, combine the cream, half-and-half, and butter. Cook over low heat until the butter is melted and small bubbles form around the edges of the pan. Remove from heat.

In a medium bowl, whisk together the eggs, sugar, vanilla, cinnamon, and orange extract. Slowly pour the egg mixture into the hot cream mixture, stirring constantly. Stir in the bread and raisins and let soak. Set aside.

In a small saucepan over medium heat, combine the apples and orange juice or water. Cover and cook until the apples are tender, about 10 minutes. Remove from heat, transfer to a medium bowl, and stir in the walnuts and brown sugar.

Arrange half of the apple mixture in the bottom of a baking dish. Add the bread mixture and top with the remaining apple mixture. Cover the baking dish with aluminum foil and bake in the preheated oven for 45 to 55 minutes, or until the center is just set.

Makes 10 servings

Crown Candy Kitchen

St. Louis, Missouri

Crown Candy Kitchen was opened in 1913 by Harry Karandzieff and Pete Jugaloff, who brought their confectionery skills with them from Greece, and today is run by Harry's descendents. They are careful to maintain the charming historical ambience of the oldest soda fountain in St. Louis, which features walls packed with turn-of-the-century memorabilia, including a huge collection of Coca-Cola trays. The lunch menu at Crown Candy includes a BLT and a Reuben sandwich, a chef's salad, and a zesty chili dog, but the real reason to visit is, of course, the soda fountain. Homemade ice cream flavorings (including Ozark Black Walnut) are blended there in an antique copper candy kettle, and the policy since 1913 has been that anyone who can drink five malts in half an hour gets them free! Living up to its name, Crown Candy Kitchen also makes nougats, peanut brittle, and chocolate figurines for every holiday.

Crown Candy Kitchen

Crown Sundae

Chocolate-Banana Malt

Lover's Delight

Crown Sundae

This sundae, developed in celebration of the St. Louis World Fair in 1904, consists of vanilla ice cream topped with hot fudge and butterscotch sauces and sprinkled with toasted pecans.

3 tablespoons hot fudge sauce (page 230)
Handful pecan halves, toasted and salted (page 234)
3 scoops vanilla ice cream
3 tablespoons butterscotch sauce (page 228)

Pour 1 tablespoon hot fudge sauce into a parfait or sundae glass, sprinkle 3 or 4 pecan halves over, and top with 2 scoops of vanilla ice cream. Drizzle 1 tablespoon butterscotch sauce over the ice cream and top with 3 or 4 more pecan halves. Add another scoop of ice cream and 1 tablespoon *each* chocolate and butterscotch sauce. Sprinkle with a few more pecan halves and serve immediately.

Makes 1 serving

Chocolate-Banana Malt

6 scoops vanilla ice cream
⅔ cup chocolate syrup
1 banana, sliced
1 cup cold milk
2 tablespoons malted milk powder

In a blender, combine all the ingredients. Blend until just mixed with a few lumps remaining. Serve at once in 2 tall glasses.

Makes 2 servings

Lover's Delight

Another authentic soda fountain treat: twin scoops of ice cream topped with crushed pineapple, strawberries, nuts, and thin slices of banana.

2 scoops vanilla ice cream

3 tablespoons sliced strawberries in juice

3 tablespoons crushed pineapple in juice

½ banana, thinly sliced

4 teaspoons nuts, crushed

¼ cup whipped cream

1 maraschino cherry

1 chocolate chip pirouette cookie

Place the ice cream in a sundae dish and spoon the strawberries and pineapple over. Top with banana slices, nuts, whipped cream, and a cherry. Serve immediately, accompanied with the cookie.

Makes 1 sundae

Daddy Maxwell's

Williams Bay, Wisconsin

Called the "Arctic Circle Diner" because of its igloo-shaped dining room, Daddy Maxwell's is well loved in Williams Bay and the surrounding area. It was originally built in the 1940s and was a drive-in, complete with carhops, in the fifties and sixties. Owners Janette and Marshall Maxwell have remodeled and expanded the diner since taking over in 1987, but have made sure that it retains its quaint personality and welcoming ambience. Specialties include hearty breakfasts such as French Batter Pancakes or homemade Biscuits with Sausage Gravy, as well as the famous Friday Night Fish Fry, accompanied with Potato Pancakes. A warm and genuine part of the community, Daddy Maxwell's serves an annual Christmas dinner for those who would otherwise be celebrating alone.

Daddy Maxwell's

Dutch Apple Monte Cristo French Batter Cake

Black-eyed Pea Soup

Mariecella's Pork Burrito with Spanish Rice

Cranberry Salad

Raisin Bars

Dutch Apple Monte Cristo French Batter Cake

A fall breakfast classic at Daddy Maxwell's.

½ tablespoon vanilla extract
2½ cups Pancake Batter (page 231)
2 tablespoons butter
3 apples, cored, peeled, and thinly sliced
½ tablespoon ground cinnamon
1 tablespoon sugar
Vegetable oil for cooking
4 thin ham slices
Grated Swiss or Cheddar cheese for sprinkling
Sifted powdered sugar for sprinkling

Stir the vanilla extract into the pancake batter. Set aside.

Meanwhile, in a large sauté pan or skillet, melt the butter over medium heat and sauté the apples, cinnamon, and sugar until the apples are soft but not mushy. Remove from heat and let cool.

Coat a large sauté pan or skillet with vegetable oil and panfry the ham slices over medium-low heat until lightly browned. Cover to keep warm and set aside. Stir the apple mixture into the pancake batter.

Preheat the oven to 250°F. Coat a large skillet with oil and heat over medium-high heat. Ladle in ½ cup of the pancake batter and cook until bubbles evenly cover the surface. Flip the pancake over and top with a ham slice and some grated cheese. When golden brown on the second side, fold the pancake in half. Transfer the pancake to a serving plate and put in the warm oven. Repeat to cook and fill the remaining pancakes. Sprinkle with powdered sugar and serve immediately.

Makes 4 servings

Black-eyed Pea Soup

Serve this Southwestern-style soup with cracked-wheat or oatmeal bread.

1 pound (about 2 cups) dried black-eyed peas, rinsed
5 quarts water
2 large smoked pork hocks or ham hocks
1 cup finely chopped onion
1 cup finely chopped celery
1 cup finely chopped peeled carrots
4 to 5 large garlic cloves, minced
1 teaspoon ground pepper
1 tablespoon salt or to taste
1 teaspoon chicken broth concentrate (optional)
1½ tablespoon minced fresh cilantro
Juice of 1 lemon

In a large soup pot, combine the black-eyed peas, water, and pork or ham hocks. Bring the liquid to a boil, reduce heat to low, and simmer for 1 hour, occasionally skimming off any foam that rises to the surface.

Stir in the onion, celery, carrots, garlic, pepper, salt, and broth concentrate, if you like. Simmer for 30 minutes, or until the peas are soft and broken up. Just before serving, stir in the cilantro and lemon juice.

Makes 12 servings

Mariecella's Pork Burrito with Spanish Rice

3 pounds lean pork, finely diced
Salt and ground black pepper to taste
2 tablespoons vegetable oil
½ cup finely diced onion
2 tablespoons minced garlic
2 green bell peppers, cored, seeded, and coarsely chopped
4 tomatoes, coarsely chopped
3 cups water
Four 8-inch flour tortillas
Spanish Rice (recipe follows)

Sprinkle the pork with salt and pepper. In a large, heavy pot over medium-high heat, heat the vegetable oil and sauté the pork, onion, and garlic until the pork is browned, about 10 minutes. Add water to cover, reduce heat to low, and simmer for 1½ hours, or until the pork is very tender; add water as necessary to prevent the meat from burning. Set aside.

In a medium saucepan, combine the green pepper, tomato, and water and bring to a boil. Cook for 10 minutes. Drain the vegetables over a bowl and add the liquid to the pork. Transfer the green pepper and tomato to a blender or food processor and blend until puréed. Stir the purée into the pork mixture and simmer until the liquid has evaporated.

In a large, dry sauté pan or skillet over high heat, warm each tortilla on both sides until pliable. Place one-fourth of the pork mixture and one-fourth of the Spanish rice in a line down the center of a tortilla, leaving a 1-inch margin at each end. Fold in the sides and roll the tortilla up from the bottom. Repeat to fill and roll the remaining tortillas. Serve immediately.

Makes 4 servings

Spanish Rice

1 tablespoon vegetable oil
1 cup long-grain white rice
1 cup water
1 cup tomato juice
½ teaspoon salt
¼ cup chopped green beans
¼ cup finely chopped peeled carrot
¼ cup finely diced peeled potato

In a large sauté pan or skillet over medium heat, heat the vegetable oil and sauté the rice until golden. Stir in the water, tomato juice, and salt. Raise heat to high, bring the liquid to a boil, and add the green beans, carrot, and potato. Reduce heat to low, cover, and simmer for 20 minutes, or until the rice and potato are tender.

Makes about 3½ cups

Cranberry Salad

One 12-ounce bag (3 cups) fresh or frozen cranberries
¾ cup sugar
One 6-ounce package cherry Jell-O
¾ cup water
1 cup green or red seedless grapes, chopped
1 cup finely chopped celery
One 14-ounce can crushed pineapple with juice
1 cup heavy (whipping) cream
2 cups miniature marshmallows

In a medium saucepan over high heat, boil the cranberries, sugar, Jell-O, and water for about 5 minutes, or until the cranberries pop. Reduce heat to low and simmer for 10 minutes. Stir in the grapes, celery, and pineapple until thoroughly combined. Pour the mixture into a 9-by-13-inch glass baking dish and refrigerate until firm.

In a deep bowl, beat the cream until stiff peaks form. Fold in the marsh-mallows. Spread the whipped cream mixture over the cranberry gelatin and serve immediately.

Makes 8 to 12 servings

Raisin Bars

2 cups raisins
1 cup (2 sticks) butter at room temperature
1 cup packed brown sugar
1¾ cups quick-cooking oats
1¾ cups all-purpose flour
1 teaspoon baking soda
1 cup sour cream
1 cup granulated sugar
3 tablespoons cornstarch
3 egg yolks
1 teaspoon vanilla extract

Preheat the oven to 350°F. In a small saucepan, combine the raisins with water to cover. Bring to a boil and cook for 2 minutes, or until the raisins plump. Drain and set aside.

In a large bowl, beat the butter and brown sugar until light and fluffy. Stir in the oatmeal, flour, and soda until thoroughly combined. Pat half of the oatmeal mixture into a 9-by-13-inch glass baking dish. Bake in the preheated oven for 10 minutes, or until set; remove from the oven and set aside.

In a small saucepan, combine the sour cream, granulated sugar, cornstarch, and egg yolks. Stir constantly over low heat until the mixture simmers. Remove from heat and stir in the vanilla and raisins.

Pour the sour cream mixture over the baked oatmeal mixture and sprinkle the remaining oatmeal mixture on top. Bake in the preheated oven for 30 minutes. Let cool and cut into squares.

Makes 18 raisin bars

The Diner

Yountville, California

Cassandra Mitchell opened The Diner in 1976 in a renovated Greyhound bus depot in California's world-famous Napa Valley. The Diner serves home-style cooking, using ingredients such as organic grains and produce from local farmer's markets, and specializes in breakfasts, traditional diner fare, Mexican food, and fresh fish. For breakfast, the highlights are delicate Cornmeal Pancakes, a Breakfast Burrito, and German Potato Pancakes served with applesauce and homemade sausage. After 5:30 p.m., The Diner becomes El Diner, focusing on Mexican and Latin American dishes as well as fresh California cuisine. Well regarded both locally and nationally for its high cooking standards and bright, happy atmosphere, The Diner lures its patrons back again and again. Cassandra Mitchell says that she's "watched kids who came into The Diner as babes-in-arms, now returning for afternoon milkshakes and a chance for an interview for that busser's job."

J. GRERIS

The Diner

Spinach Quesadillas with Avocado Salsa

Scrambled Eggs and Sautéed Peppers on Tortillas

Lemon Piccata Chicken on Focaccia Bread

Pumpkin-Ginger Flan

Spinach Quesadillas with Avocado Salsa

A savory appetizer with an unusual salsa topping. Patrons of The Diner often eat a whole quesadilla as a light meal.

Filling
1 tablespoon chopped pickled jalapeño
2 garlic cloves
1 bunch fresh spinach, stemmed
1 cup (4 ounces) grated Asiago cheese
½ cup (2 ounces) grated Monterey jack cheese

Garlic Butter
4 tablespoons butter at room temperature
2 garlic cloves, minced

4 flour tortillas
Avocado Salsa (recipe follows)

To make the filling: In a blender or food processor, chop the jalapeño and garlic. Add the remaining filling ingredients and blend to a paste.

To make the garlic butter: In a small bowl, blend the garlic and butter together.

Spread the tortillas with the garlic butter. Spread the spinach mixture evenly over 2 of the tortillas and top them with the other 2 tortillas. In a large skillet over medium heat, cook the tortillas until they are golden brown and the cheese melts. Cut into wedges, top with avocado salsa, and serve immediately.

Makes 2 quesadillas (12 appetizers)

Avocado Salsa

1 avocado, peeled, pitted, and cut into ½-inch cubes
1 tablespoon minced onion
1 tablespoon minced fresh cilantro
2 tablespoons seasoned rice vinegar
1 tablespoon apple cider vinegar
¼ teaspoon salt

In a medium bowl, gently mix together all the ingredients.

Makes about 1 cup salsa

Scrambled Eggs and Sautéed Peppers on Tortillas

Salsa
2 tomatoes, peeled, seeded, and chopped (page 232)
1 garlic clove, minced
2 green onions, white part only, sliced
1 tablespoon fresh lime juice
2 tablespoons minced fresh cilantro
¼ teaspoon salt
¼ teaspoon ground pepper

Garnish
2 oranges
Juice of ½ lemon
1½ avocados, peeled, quartered, and pitted

2 tablespoons vegetable oil
2 Anaheim or poblano chilies, cored, seeded, and cut into 1-inch dice
1 *each* red and yellow bell pepper, cored, seeded, and cut into 1-inch dice

2 onions, chopped

6 large garlic cloves, sliced

1 pickled jalapeño chili, minced (optional)

⅓ cup chicken stock (page 228) or canned low-salt chicken broth

3 tablespoons minced fresh cilantro

Six 8-inch flour tortillas

2 tablespoons butter

12 eggs, beaten

8 ounces feta cheese, crumbled (1½ cups)

To make the salsa: In a small bowl, combine the tomatoes, garlic, green onions, and lime juice. Stir in the cilantro, salt, and pepper and set aside. (The salsa may be covered with plastic wrap and refrigerated up to 4 hours before serving.)

To make the garnish: Cut off the orange peels down to the flesh. Cut the oranges into thin crosswise slices. Squeeze the lemon juice over the avocados. (The avocados may be covered with plastic wrap and refrigerated for up to 4 hours.)

In a large sauté pan or skillet over medium heat, heat the vegetable oil and sauté the chili, bell peppers, and onions until tender and beginning to brown, about 10 minutes. Add the garlic and pickled jalapeño, if using, and sauté 2 minutes longer. Stir in the chicken stock or broth and cilantro, raise heat to high, and bring the liquid to a boil. Cover and cook for 2 to 3 minutes. Drain and discard the liquid. (The bell pepper mixture may be cooled, covered, and refrigerated overnight at this point.)

Preheat the oven to 200°F. Wrap the tortillas in a damp kitchen towel and heat them on the bottom rack of the oven until warm, about 10 minutes.

To make the avocado fans, start at the base of each avocado quarter and thinly slice the avocado lengthwise to within 1 inch of the tip. Gently spread the slices to make fans.

In a large sauté pan or skillet, melt the butter over medium heat and sauté the pepper mixture until heated through. Pour in the eggs and cook, stirring

113

constantly, for 4 minutes, or until set but still soft. Transfer the tortillas to 6 warmed dinner plates. Top each tortilla with 2 tablespoons of salsa, then some eggs. Sprinkle the eggs with feta cheese and garnish with avocado fans and orange slices. Serve immediately.

Makes 6 servings

Lemon Piccata Chicken on Focaccia Bread

Sauce
⅓ cup fresh lemon juice
1 tablespoon soy sauce
1 tablespoon caper juice
1 teaspoon sugar
½ cup water

1 cup all-purpose flour
½ teaspoon salt
½ teaspoon ground black pepper
2 whole chicken breasts, skinned, boned, and pounded ¼ inch thick
¼ cup olive oil
2 tablespoons slivered garlic
1 tablespoon grated lemon zest
¼ cup capers, drained
One 8-by-12-inch focaccia bread
Roasted red bell peppers (page 234) for topping (optional)
Sliced onions for topping (optional)

To make the sauce: In a small bowl, whisk together the lemon juice, soy sauce, caper juice, sugar, and water.

In a shallow dish, mix the flour, salt, and pepper together. Dredge the chicken in the seasoned flour until well coated.

In a large sauté pan or skillet over medium heat, heat the olive oil and sauté the chicken until lightly browned on both sides. Remove the chicken with tongs, let cool, and slice; set aside. In the same pan over medium heat, sauté the garlic for 45 seconds, then stir in the lemon zest and capers. Stir in the sauce, raise heat to high, and cook to reduce the liquid by two thirds.

Cut the focaccia bread into 2 layers. Arrange the chicken over the bottom layer of the focaccia and spread the sauce over the the cut side of the top layer. Add a layer of roasted peppers and onions, if desired. Top with the second layer of focaccia.

Cut the sandwich into 1½-inch squares for appetizer portions or 2 to 3 larger sections for main-course portions.

Makes 6 to 8 appetizers, or 2 to 3 main-course sandwiches

Pumpkin-Ginger Flan

A delicious twist on traditional flan that's good any time of the year.

Caramel
1 cup sugar
½ cup water
¼ cup grated peeled fresh ginger

Flan
1 cup milk
1 cup half-and-half
3 eggs
2 egg yolks
1½ cups canned pumpkin
⅓ cup sugar
¼ teaspoon salt

Preheat the oven to 325°F. To make the caramel: In a small, heavy skillet, cook the sugar over medium heat until golden; be careful not to burn it. Add the water and ginger and cook over low heat just until golden brown, 8 to 10 minutes. Strain the caramel through a fine-meshed sieve into a bowl; reserve the ginger. Ladle about 2 tablespoons of the hot caramel into each of eight 6-ounce custard cups or ramekins. Swirl the caramel to coat the inside of the containers.

To make the flan: In a medium, heavy saucepan, heat the milk and half-and-half over low heat until small bubbles form around the edges of the pan. Meanwhile, beat the eggs and egg yolks together in a medium bowl. Remove the milk mixture from heat. Whisk ½ cup of the milk mixture into the beaten eggs, then gradually add the remaining milk mixture. Stir in the pumpkin, sugar, salt, and the reserved ginger until well blended. Ladle ½ cup of the custard into each of the 8 cups or ramekins.

Place the containers in a baking dish and pour hot water into the dish to halfway up the sides of the containers. Bake in the preheated oven for 45 minutes, or until the custards are set but still quiver in the center. Remove the containers from the hot water and let cool. Serve at room temperature.

Makes 8 custards

Dutch Kitchen Restaurant

Frackville, Pennsylvania

Although it's called a restaurant, there is no disguising the fact that the Dutch Kitchen is a diner through and through. The outside has been bricked over and a wood-paneled dining room attached, but when you enter, the diner configuration is classic: a double counter where customers can get a good view of the pie cases, red Naugahyde booths looking out over Route 61, a roof still showing pink Formica, and the aroma of fresh coffee in the air. This is Pennsylvania coal-mining country, and Dutch Kitchen customers appreciate the rib-sticking qualities of Dutch Meat Loaf with rich gravy, the juicy Distleburger (a cheeseburger with sautéed mushrooms), and Pennsylvania-style Chicken Pot Pie, served with a big dish of applesauce.

Dutch Kitchen Restaurant

Chicken Pot Pie

Dutch Meat Loaf

Deep-Dish Apple Pie

Chicken Pot Pie

This Pennsylvania-style pot pie is more like a hearty stew of dumplings, chicken, and vegetables cooked in broth. At the Dutch Kitchen, it is served with a dish of homemade applesauce (page 225).

One 4-pound chicken, cut up

12 cups water

1½ teaspoons salt

½ teaspoon ground pepper

1 celery stalk, finely diced

4 new red potatoes (about 1 pound), peeled and quartered

1 onion, coarsely chopped

4 carrots, peeled and cut into 1-inch disks

2 tablespoons minced fresh parsley

Dumplings

2 cups all-purpose flour

½ teaspoon salt

1 teaspoon baking powder

2 tablespoons vegetable shortening

1 egg, beaten

⅓ cup water

In a large pot, combine the chicken, water, salt, pepper, and celery; bring to a boil. Reduce heat to low and simmer for 1 hour, occasionally skimming any foam that rises to the surface. Remove the chicken from the pot and let cool slightly. Remove the meat from the bones, discarding the skin. Return the meat to the pot and add the potatoes, onion, and carrots. Bring to a boil, reduce heat to a simmer, and cook for 20 minutes. Stir in the parsley.

Meanwhile, prepare the dumplings: In a medium bowl, stir together the flour, salt, and baking powder. Cut in the vegetable shortening with a pastry cutter or 2 knives until the mixture is as fine as cracker meal. Stir in the egg and water with a fork until the dough forms a mass. Or, process the flour, salt,

119

baking powder, and vegetable shortening in a food processor until the mixture is as fine as cracker meal. Add the egg and water and process until the mixture forms a mass.

On a lightly floured board, roll out the dough to a ⅛-inch thickness. Cut it into 2-inch squares. Drop the squares into the boiling chicken and vegetables. Cover the pot and cook the dumplings for 15 to 20 minutes, or until tender and puffed. Serve in shallow soup bowls.

Makes 6 servings

Dutch Meat Loaf

Stout comfort food served with creamy mashed potatoes, brown gravy, and boiled carrots at the Dutch Kitchen.

1 pound lean ground beef
1 cup dried bread crumbs
1 egg, beaten
¼ cup finely chopped onion
¼ cup finely chopped celery
1 teaspoon salt
¼ teaspoon ground pepper
Brown gravy (page 227)
Mashed potatoes (page 231)

Preheat the oven to 350°F. In a large bowl, mix all the ingredients except the gravy and the mashed potatoes together until well blended. Pat the mixture into a 9-by-5-inch loaf pan. Bake in the preheated oven for 1½ hours, or until browned and firm to the touch. Let cool for 15 minutes before slicing and serving.

Makes 4 to 6 servings

Deep-Dish Apple Pie

Delicious served warm and topped with ice cream or whipped cream and a sprinkling of cinnamon-sugar.

1 recipe Pie Pastry dough, chilled (page 232)

1 cup sugar

⅓ cup all-purpose flour

1 teaspoon ground nutmeg

1 teaspoon ground cinnamon

Dash of salt

8 tart apples, such as pippin or Granny Smith, peeled, cored, and
   thinly sliced (about 8 cups)

3 tablespoons butter, cut into small pieces

Topping

Ice cream or whipped cream

2 teaspoons sugar

¼ teaspoon ground cinnamon

Preheat the oven to 425°F. On a lightly floured work surface, roll out half of the dough to form a circle ⅛ inch thick. Fit into a 10-inch pie plate and trim the dough, leaving a 1-inch overhang. Roll out the top crust.

In a large bowl, mix the sugar, flour, nutmeg, cinnamon, and salt together. Add the apples and toss until thoroughly combined. Pour the apple mixture into the prepared pie shell, mounding it slightly. Dot with butter, cover with the top crust, and crimp the edges. Cut some steam vents and bake the pie in the preheated oven for 40 to 50 minutes, or until golden brown. Let cool slightly. Cut into wedges and serve with ice cream or whipped cream. Stir the sugar and cinnamon until well blended and sprinkle it over the ice cream or whipped cream.

Makes one 10-inch pie

11th Street Diner

Miami Beach, Florida

The 11th Street Diner is an original Art Deco–style diner from Wilkes-Barre, Pennsylvania. Built in 1948 by the Paramount Dining Car Company of Haledon, New Jersey, it was transported to Wilkes-Barre, where it opened that year. Traditional American food was served there for forty-four years, before the diner was dismantled and transported to the historic Art Deco district of Miami Beach. After months of restoration, Ray and Steren Schnitzer opened the diner again in 1992. Voted Best Late-Night Eatery by the *New Times* in 1994, it serves traditional diner fare and contemporary gourmet cooking twenty-four hours a day, seven days a week.

11th Street Diner

Yankee Pot Roast

Chicken Fettuccine

Potato Pancakes

Key Lime Pie

Yankee Pot Roast

5 pounds beef bottom round roast, trimmed of fat
Salt and freshly ground pepper to taste
Flour for dusting, plus ¼ cup all-purpose flour
2 tablespoons vegetable oil
½ cup finely diced peeled carrot
½ cup finely chopped onion
½ cup finely diced celery
½ cup red wine vinegar
2 tablespoons sweet Hungarian paprika
2 tablespoons tomato paste
2 bay leaves
3 garlic cloves
¼ cup A-1 sauce
½ cup cold water

Sprinkle the pot roast with salt and pepper and dust with flour. In a Dutch oven or large, heavy pot over medium heat, heat the vegetable oil and brown the meat on all sides. Remove the meat from the pan. Reduce heat to low and stir in all the remaining ingredients except the water. Return the meat to the pan and add water to cover the meat. Cook over low heat for 3 to 3½ hours, or until the meat is very tender.

Transfer the meat to a cutting board and cover it loosely with aluminum foil. Skim the fat from the liquid in the pot. Mix the ½ cup water and flour to make a smooth paste. Return the pot to high heat and gradually whisk in the flour mixture. Cook for about 5 minutes, or until thickened, stirring constantly. Taste and adjust the seasoning.

Cut the meat into thick slices and place them on warm plates. Pour some of the gravy over and serve.

Makes 8 servings

Chicken Fettuccine

1 tablespoon salt
8 ounces fresh or dried fettuccine
1 tablespoon butter
1 teaspoon minced garlic
½ cup sliced mushrooms
1 skinless, boneless chicken breast half, cut into 1-inch cubes
¼ cup dry white wine
½ cup heavy (whipping) cream
½ cup (2 ounces) grated Parmesan cheese
Cracked black pepper for garnish
Minced fresh parsley for garnish

Bring a large pot of water to a boil. Add the salt, then the fettuccine, and cook until al dente.

Meanwhile, in a medium sauté pan or skillet, melt the butter over medium heat and sauté the garlic, mushrooms, and chicken for 3 to 4 minutes, or until the chicken is lightly browned. Stir in the white wine and cream and bring to a boil. Remove the pan from heat and stir in the Parmesan cheese.

Drain the fettuccine, put it in a warm serving bowl, and toss with the chicken mixture. Sprinkle with pepper and parsley and serve immediately.

Makes 2 servings

Potato Pancakes

Serve these crisp potato pancakes with homemade applesauce (page 225).

6 Idaho potatoes, peeled
2 white onions
¼ teaspoon salt
¼ teaspoon ground pepper
3 eggs, lightly beaten
½ bunch fresh parsley, stemmed and minced
1 tablespoon grated Parmesan cheese
2 cups all-purpose flour
Vegetable oil for frying

Preheat the oven to 250°F. Using a hand grater or food processor, shred the potatoes and onions separately. Squeeze the potatoes in batches in a muslin cloth to remove as much water as possible. In a large bowl, combine the potatoes, onions, and all the remaining ingredients except the oil and stir until thoroughly mixed. Shape into 8 patties.

In a large sauté pan or skillet over medium-high heat, heat ⅛ inch vegetable oil and cook a few of the pancakes 1½ to 2 minutes on each side, or until golden brown. Using a slotted spatula, transfer the pancakes to a baking sheet and place the pan in the warm oven. Repeat to cook the remaining pancakes, adding more oil as needed. Serve immediately.

Makes 8 servings

Key Lime Pie

¼ cup fresh lime juice, preferably from Key limes
One 7-ounce can sweetened condensed milk
½ cup heavy (whipping) cream
One 9-inch graham cracker pie crust (page 230)
1 teaspoon grated lime zest

In a medium bowl, combine the lime juice and sweetened condensed milk and blend thoroughly. In a deep bowl, whip the heavy cream until stiff peaks form. Fold the whipped cream into the milk mixture. Spoon the filling into the prepared shell. Sprinkle with the lime zest and refrigerate, uncovered, until firm, 2 to 3 hours.

Makes one 9-inch pie; serves 8

Empire Diner

New York, New York

The Empire Diner, manufactured by the Fodero Dining Car Company in 1946, was taken over in 1976 by Jack Doenias and his partners, who modified it to appeal to an upscale New York crowd. The 15-by-51-foot diner still has the Fodero-trademark winged clock above its coffee urns and the original stainless steel interior, but the Formica counter and tabletops have been replaced with black glass, a miniature stainless steel Empire State building is installed on the roof, and a giant sign saying "EAT" now beckons customers from the wall behind the building. Pioneering the concept of a diner being something more than just a diner, the Empire features candlelit dining, live jazz piano music, a great beer and cocktail list, and an untraditional menu by chef Mitchell R. Woo. An instant success, the Empire has received wide national attention that has furthered the popularity of diners—Heinz even used its image in an ad campaign for their ketchup. Famous customers have included Marvin Hamlisch, Barbara Streisand, and Steven Spielberg.

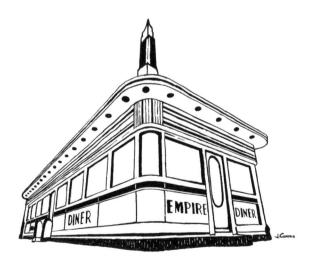

Empire Diner

Chinese Trout in Filo

Sautéed Chicken Breasts Mirabeau

Empire Meat Loaf

Empire Mashed Potatoes

Calves' Liver with Cream and Blueberries

Poached Pears in Wine

Chinese Trout in Filo

Serve this dish with snow peas and steamed white or brown rice.

Six 8-ounce boneless trout, rinsed and patted dry

8 ounces filo sheets, thawed

¾ cup peanut oil

¼ cup dry sherry

1 tablespoon Asian sesame oil

2 garlic cloves, minced

1 tablespoon minced fresh ginger

¼ teaspoon ground pepper

4 to 5 green onions, including some green tops, finely cut on the diagonal

2 tablespoons sesame seeds

Dipping Sauce

¾ cup soy sauce

¼ cup plain rice wine vinegar

¼ cup Asian sesame oil

Cut off the head, tail, side fins, and collar fins of each trout. Place a trout, skin-side down, on a flat surface. Using a very sharp knife, cut the trout in half lengthwise and remove the spine. Repeat with the remaining trout to make 12 fillets with the skin on.

Working quickly, place 1 filo sheet on a work surface with the short end closest to you; brush lightly with peanut oil. Cover the unused filo with a damp kitchen towel to keep it from drying out. Align another sheet of filo on top of the first and brush with more peanut oil. Repeat until you have 5 oiled sheets of filo stacked up.

In a medium bowl, whisk together the sherry, sesame oil, garlic, ginger, and pepper. Dip 2 trout fillets in the sherry mixture, drain off the excess, and lay the fillets on top of each other head to tail. Place the doubled fillets on top of the stack of filo, parallel to and ½ inch from the edge of the stack closest to you. (This makes a fish sandwich of uniform thickness that will cook evenly.) Sprinkle with green onions and sesame seeds.

Fold the edge of the stack over the fillets and roll the filo and fish over so that the trout is covered with 5 layers of filo. Fold in the long sides of the filo and continue rolling the filo and trout to make a flat packet. Brush the top lightly with peanut oil and place, seam-side down, on a lightly oiled baking sheet. Repeat with the other trout fillets and filo. Cover and refrigerate for 30 minutes.

Meanwhile, preheat the oven to 450°F. Place the filo rolls in the preheated oven and bake for 6 to 8 minutes, or until the pastry is golden and flaky.

Meanwhile, to make the dipping sauce: In a medium bowl, whisk together all the ingredients. Serve 1 packet on each of 6 warm plates, accompanied with a small bowl of dipping sauce.

Makes 6 servings

Sautéed Chicken Breasts Mirabeau

Serve this dish with couscous and a broiled tomato half.

4 boneless, skinless chicken breast halves
Flour for dredging
2 eggs beaten with ¼ cup water
¼ cup peanut oil
5 ounces mushrooms, sliced
½ cup dry sherry
8 cooked or thawed frozen large artichoke hearts, quartered (page 225)
24 black olives, pitted and sliced
2 teaspoons minced fresh thyme
2 teaspoons minced fresh oregano

2 teaspoons minced fresh sage
4 teaspoons minced fresh Italian parsley
4 tablespoons butter

Preheat the oven to 250°F. Using the flat side of a meat mallet or the bottom of a heavy bottle, pound the chicken breasts to a uniform ¼-inch thickness. Dredge the chicken in the flour, then in the egg mixture.

In a large sauté pan or skillet over medium-high heat, heat the peanut oil and sauté the chicken breasts until browned on both sides. Reduce heat to low and cook for a total of 8 to 10 minutes, turning once, or until the chicken is springy to the touch. Transfer the chicken to a plate and put it in the warm oven.

Pour all but 1 tablespoon of the oil from the pan and increase the heat to medium. Add the mushrooms and sauté for 2 to 3 minutes. Add the sherry and cook for 3 minutes, stirring to scrape up the browned bits from the bottom of the pan. Add the artichokes and black olives and toss to heat thoroughly. Stir in the thyme, oregano, sage, parsley, and any juices from the plate holding the chicken breasts. Remove the pan from heat, add the butter, and swirl it until melted.

Dip the chicken breasts in the sauce and arrange them on each of 4 plates. Pour the sauce over and serve.

Makes 4 servings

Empire Meat Loaf

6 ounces bulk pork sausage

¼ cup mayonnaise

⅓ cup oyster sauce (available in Asian markets and some grocery stores)

Half of one 10-ounce package frozen chopped spinach, thawed and
    squeezed dry

½ onion, finely chopped

1 teaspoon minced garlic

Pinch ground nutmeg

¾ teaspoon ground pepper

¼ cup rolled oats

1½ pounds ground beef

½ tablespoon butter

¼ cup minced shallots

6 cups veal stock, beef stock (page 226), or canned low-salt beef broth

Bovril beef concentrate to taste (optional)

Cherry tomatoes and glazed baby carrots for garnish

Empire Mashed Potatoes (recipe follows)

Preheat the oven to 350°F. Grease a 9-by-5-inch loaf pan. Crumble the sausage into a cold medium sauté pan or skillet and place the pan over medium heat; cook the sausage until it is no longer pink, breaking it up with a fork. Drain and discard the fat. Set the cooked sausage aside to cool to room temperature.

In a large bowl, mix together the mayonnaise, oyster sauce, spinach, onion, garlic, nutmeg, pepper, and oats until thoroughly combined. Mix the sausage into the mayonnaise mixture. Add the ground beef and mix just until blended. Pat the meat mixture into a loaf at least 3 inches high and place in the prepared loaf pan.

Cover the loaf with greased parchment paper or aluminum foil and bake in the preheated oven for 1 hour. Pour off any fat and bake another 20 to 30 minutes, or the meat loaf is browned and firm, and a meat thermometer inserted in the center reads 155°F. Set the meat loaf aside to cool slightly.

In a sauté pan or skillet, melt the butter over medium heat and sauté the shallots until translucent, about 3 minutes. Set aside.

In a medium nonaluminum saucepan cook the stock or broth over high heat to reduce to 1½ cups. Add the optional beef concentrate, ½ teaspoon at a time, until the sauce has a strong, rich flavor. Add the shallots and simmer gently for 3 to 4 minutes.

Transfer the meat loaf to a serving platter and cut it into ½-inch-thick slices. Dribble some of the sauce over and garnish the platter with cherry tomatoes and glazed baby carrots. Serve with mashed potatoes and pass the sauce separately.

Makes 6 servings

Empire Mashed Potatoes

The potatoes may be reheated in a microwave, but they are best served right away. No need to top with butter.

2 pounds unpeeled red new potatoes, scrubbed
¼ teaspoon salt
¼ cup milk, heated
¼ cup heavy (whipping) cream, heated
¼ cup chicken stock (page 228), vegetable stock, or
     canned low-salt chicken broth, heated
¼ tablespoon ground pepper
2 tablespoons snipped fresh chives
4 tablespoons unsalted butter

Place the potatoes in a large pot and add water to cover by 2 inches. Bring to a boil, add the salt, reduce heat to low, and simmer for 20 minutes, or until the potatoes are tender. Remove from heat and drain well.

In a large bowl, mash the potatoes well with a hand-held electric mixer or a potato masher. Beat in the milk, cream, stock or broth, pepper, and chives, scraping down the sides of the bowl with a rubber spatula. Stir in the butter until it has melted. Serve immediately.

Makes 6 servings

Calves' Liver with Cream and Blueberries

Serve this dish with roast potatoes and grilled or steamed summer squash.

1 pound calves' liver, cut into ¼-inch-thick slices
Flour for dredging
4 tablespoons peanut oil
¼ cup minced shallots
½ cup dry sherry
1 cup apple juice
1⅓ cups half-and-half
1⅓ cups fresh blueberries

Preheat the oven to 250°F. Dredge the liver slices in flour. In a large sauté pan or skillet over medium heat, heat 2 tablespoons of the peanut oil and sauté half of the liver, turning once, until the liver is springy to the touch, a total of 2 minutes. Transfer the liver to a platter and place it in the warm oven. Repeat to cook the remaining half of the liver.

Pour off all but 1 tablespoon of oil from the pan and sauté the shallots for 2 minutes, or until translucent. Stir in the sherry and apple juice, raise heat to high, and cook to reduce the liquid by half. Reduce the heat to low, stir in the half-and-half, and simmer until it thickens slightly.

Return the liver slices to the pan and turn them over in the sauce. Transfer the liver to 4 warmed serving plates. Turn off heat, add the blueberries to the sauce, and swirl gently until the berries just start to color the sauce. Pour the sauce and berries over the liver.

Makes 4 servings

Poached Pears in Wine

1½ cups dry red or dry white wine
½ lemon, thinly sliced
1 cup plus 2 tablespoons sugar
½ cinnamon stick
Pinch of freshly grated nutmeg
4 firm ripe pears
Lightly sweetened freshly whipped cream for garnish

In a large nonaluminum saucepan, combine the wine, lemon, sugar, cinnamon stick, and nutmeg. Simmer over medium heat until the sugar dissolves, stirring occasionally. Peel the pears, leaving the stems on, and add them to the pan. Cover, reduce heat to low, and simmer for 20 to 35 minutes, or until the pears are tender.

Using a slotted spoon, transfer the pears to a bowl. Strain the poaching liquid and return it to the pan. Boil the liquid over high heat until the sauce is thick enough to coat the back of a spoon. Pour the sauce over the pears and refrigerate until chilled.

To serve, place a pear on each of 4 plates, spoon some syrup over, and garnish with a little whipped cream.

Makes 4 servings

4th Street Diner

Newport, Rhode Island

The 4th Street Diner is a 1950 O'Mahony diner that was originally located in Swansea, Massachusetts. In 1967, it was moved to its current location in Newport, Rhode Island, where it was purchased and restored by Tish Warner in 1989. The diner sits beside the one remaining railroad track in Newport, which replaced Newport's Fourth Street in the 1880s. A full-service grill behind the front counter offers a glimpse of the art of the true "grill man," though since 4th Street is run by Warner and her daughters, the grill man is more likely to be a woman! Warner is a fierce lover of "the diner principle" and strives to retain the old-fashioned feeling of comfort and community that was the soul of the original diners. As a result, customers return to the 4th Street Diner as much for its warm, friendly atmosphere as for its mouth-watering homemade mashed potatoes, roast turkey, meat loaf, soups, pies, and puddings.

4th Street Diner

Portuguese Kale Soup

French Meat Pie

Death by Chocolate

Portuguese Kale Soup

2 tablespoons vegetable oil

2 pounds boneless stewing beef, cut into 1-inch cubes

2 pounds chorizo or other spicy sausage, cut into ¼-inch-thick slices

2 potatoes, peeled and cubed

One 27-ounce can kidney beans, drained

2 onions, cut into 1-inch dice

½ cabbage, cored and cut into 1-inch dice

1 teaspoon red pepper flakes

1 bunch kale, torn into 2- to 3-inch pieces

Beef stock (page 226) or canned low-salt beef broth to taste

Salt to taste

In a large, heavy pot over medium heat, heat the oil and sauté the stew meat and sausage for 10 minutes, or until browned on all sides. Add water to cover. Cover and simmer over low heat for 1½ to 2 hours, or until the meat is tender; occasionally skim off any foam that rises to the surface. Stir in the potatoes, kidney beans, onions, cabbage, and red pepper flakes and cook until the vegetables are tender, about 15 minutes. Add the kale and cook for 5 to 10 minutes, or until the kale is tender. Add the beef stock or broth and salt. Serve hot.

Makes 8 servings

French Meat Pie

1 pound lean ground beef

1 pound bulk sausage

1 onion, finely chopped

1 cup beef stock (page 226) or canned low salt beef broth

1 cup mashed potatoes (page 231)

Salt and freshly ground pepper to taste

1 recipe pie pastry, chilled (page 232)

1 egg, beaten

Preheat the oven to 350°F. In a large sauté pan or skillet, sauté the ground beef over medium heat until browned. Using a slotted spoon, transfer the beef to a bowl. Pour off the fat from the pan.

In the same pan, sauté the sausage for 10 minutes, or until browned. Pour off all but 1 tablespoon of the fat. Add the onion and sauté for 5 minutes, or until translucent. Remove the pan from heat and stir in the hamburger, stock or broth, mashed potatoes, salt, and pepper; the mixture should be moist but firm.

On a lightly floured surface, roll out the pastry to make two 11-inch circles. Fit 1 circle into a 10-inch pie shell. Pour in the meat filling. Cover with the second pastry circle and seal the edges. Cut in steam vents and brush with the beaten egg. Bake in the preheated oven for 45 minutes, or until golden brown. Let cool slightly, cut into wedges, and serve.

Makes 8 to 10 servings

Death by Chocolate

¾ cup heavy (whipping) cream, plus more for topping
1 recipe Brownies, crumbled into small pieces (page 227)
2 cups Chocolate Mousse (page 229)
1 bag Heath bars, broken into pieces

In a deep bowl, beat the heavy cream until soft peaks form. Reserve ½ cup of the whipped cream for topping; cover and refrigerate.

In a large bowl, arrange one-third of the crumbled brownies and spread one-third of the chocolate mousse on top. Sprinkle over one-third of the candy pieces and top with one-third of the remaining whipped cream. Repeat the layers, ending with whipped cream. Refrigerate the dessert for at least 1 hour before serving. Serve large spoonfuls topped with some of the reserved cream.

Highland Park Diner

Rochester, New York

Included in the Rochester Landmark Society's list of significant architectural gems, the Highland Park Diner was built by the Orleans Company on site in 1948 and is believed to be the only diner made by that firm still in existence—only three or four were manufactured before the company went bankrupt. The building functioned as a diner from 1948 to 1974, was vacant for two years, then became an off-track betting parlor run by New York State. In 1986, owner Bob Malley bought the building, renovated it, and opened it as a diner once again. Today Highland Park patrons range from college students to older couples, all of whom enjoy the diner's traditional foods as well as its "new-fashioned" dishes. Emphasizing freshness, the menu features mashed potatoes, hamburgers, homemade soups, freshly squeezed orange juice, and a truly delicious apple pie (selected as best in the United States by *Condé Nast Traveler*). The diner seats fifty-five, nineteen at the counter and thirty-six at the booths.

Highland Park Diner

Cucumber Vichyssoise

Highland Park Diner Meat Loaf

Rochester-Style Barbecue Sauce

Black Forest Cheesecake

Cucumber Vichyssoise

4 tablespoons butter
3 cups diced unpeeled cucumbers
1½ cups thinly sliced leeks (white part only)
1 potato, peeled and diced
3 tablespoons chicken stock (page 228) or canned low-salt chicken broth
½ cup minced fresh parsley
1 cup heavy (whipping) cream
1 teaspoon salt
⅛ teaspoon ground white pepper
Snipped fresh chives for garnish

In a large sauté pan or skillet, melt the butter over low heat and sauté the cucumbers and leeks for 10 minutes, or until the leeks are tender. Stir in the potato, chicken stock or broth, and parsley. Cover and simmer for 20 minutes, or until the vegetables are tender. Remove the soup from heat and let cool. Transfer to a blender or food processor and purée, in batches if necessary. Stir in the cream, salt, and pepper. Refrigerate the soup until chilled. Ladle into soup bowls and garnish with chives.

Makes 6 servings

Highland Park Diner Meat Loaf

Chef Dan Judy's meat loaf is one of the most popular items on the Highland Park Diner menu.

2 pounds ground sirloin or ground chuck
1 green pepper, cored, seeded, and finely chopped
1 onion, finely chopped
2 eggs, beaten
¼ cup A-1 steak sauce
½ tablespoon Worcestershire sauce
½ cup fresh bread crumbs
Half of a 10¾-ounce can mushroom soup
¾ teaspoon garlic powder
¾ teaspoon onion powder
¾ teaspoon ground pepper

Preheat the oven to 350°F. In a large bowl, mix all of the ingredients together until well blended. Pat the mixture into a 9-by-5-inch loaf pan and bake in the preheated oven for 1 hour, or until browned and firm to the touch. Let cool for about 10 minutes before slicing and serving.

Makes 8 to 10 servings

Rochester-Style Barbecue Sauce

A great sauce for grilled pork or chicken.

4 tablespoons butter

1½ cups plain (not smoked) barbecue sauce

1 cup red hot sauce

½ cup honey

1 tablespoon Worcestershire sauce

1 teaspoon cayenne pepper

1 teaspoon red pepper flakes

1 teaspoon Tabasco sauce

In a large saucepan, melt the butter over medium heat. Stir in all of the remaining ingredients and bring to a boil. Let cool.

Makes about 3 cups

Black Forest Cheesecake

1½ cups crushed chocolate graham crackers

6 tablespoons butter at room temperature

½ tablespoon almond extract

10 ounces semisweet chocolate, chopped

Four 8-ounce packages cream cheese at room temperature

3 eggs

⅔ cup sugar

⅓ cup milk

Three 21-ounce cans cherry pie filling

Juice of 1 lemon

Preheat the oven to 350°F. In a medium bowl, mix together the graham crackers, butter, and almond extract. Press the graham cracker mixture into the bottom of a 9-by-3-inch springform pan.

In a double boiler over barely simmering water, melt the chocolate, stirring frequently. Set aside.

In a large bowl, using an electric mixer at low speed, beat the cream cheese until smooth. Add the melted chocolate, eggs, sugar, and milk and beat until well blended. Increase the mixer speed to medium and beat for 3 minutes, occasionally scraping down the sides of the bowl with a rubber spatula.

Pour the cream cheese mixture into the prepared pan. Place the pan on a baking sheet and bake the cheesecake in the preheated oven for 45 minutes, or until set. Let cool on a wire rack. Cover with plastic wrap and refrigerate the cheesecake at least 4 hours or overnight.

In a medium bowl, stir together the cherry pie filling and lemon juice; refrigerate until chilled.

To serve, carefully remove the sides of the tart pan. Cut the cheesecake into 12 pieces and serve each with a large dollop of pie filling.

Makes 12 servings

Jigger's Diner

East Greenwich, Rhode Island

Jigger's Diner has been a fixture in East Greenwich in some form as far back as 1917, when Vilgot A. "Jigger" Lindberg began his first diner business as Lindy's. Later renamed Jigger's, it functioned as a diner until 1983, when it was closed and used to store paint. Carol Shriner bought the diner and began restoration in 1992. For six months, Shriner (a former biochemist at Brown University) and her crew worked hard to bring this Worcester Lunch Car back to life, stripping wood, saving original fixtures, and locating replacement equipment and booths from other old diners. With its original luster now restored, Jigger's is blue, accented with stainless steel on the outside and mahogany and ceramic tiles on the inside. In addition to tasty specialties like johnnycakes and turkey croquettes, Shriner serves made-from-scratch sausage patties and corned beef hash, hearty soups, wonderful muffins and pastries, and homemade ice cream.

Jigger's Diner

Gingerbread Pancakes

Pumpkin Pancakes

Fancy French Toast Club Sandwich

Home Fries

Cheese Omelette

Apple, Onion, and Cheddar Omelette

Italian Omelette

Gingerbread Pancakes

Drizzle the pancakes with warm maple syrup and top with fresh blueberries or a dollop of applesauce.

1 cup freshly brewed hot coffee
½ cup packed brown sugar
1 egg
4 tablespoons butter, melted
½ cup whole-wheat flour
½ cup all-purpose flour
¾ teaspoon baking soda
½ teaspoon ground ginger
½ teaspoon ground cinnamon
¼ teaspoon ground cloves
¼ teaspoon salt
Vegetable oil for cooking
Warm maple syrup for serving
Fresh blueberries or homemade applesauce (page 225) for serving

Preheat the oven to 250°F. In a large bowl, stir together the coffee and sugar until the sugar is dissolved. Beat in the egg and melted butter until thoroughly combined.

In a medium bowl, combine the flour, baking soda, ginger, cinnamon, cloves, and salt and stir until well mixed. Add the flour mixture to the coffee mixture and stir together just until blended.

Heat a large skillet over medium-high heat and add just enough oil to coat the pan. Pour ⅛ cup batter for each pancake. Do not crowd the pan. When the pancakes are covered with bubbles, turn them and cook on the second side until browned on the bottom. Using a metal spatula, transfer the pancakes to serving plates and put them in the warm oven. Repeat to cook the remaining pancakes. To serve, drizzle the pancakes with maple syrup and a sprinkling of blueberries or a dollop of applesauce.

Makes 4 large pancakes

Pumpkin Pancakes

1 cup all-purpose flour
2 tablespoons sugar
2 teaspoons baking soda
½ teaspoon salt
½ teaspoon ground cinnamon
1 cup milk
½ cup canned pumpkin
2 egg yolks
2 tablespoons butter, melted
2 egg whites, stiffly beaten
Vegetable oil for cooking

Preheat the oven to 250°F. In a large bowl, combine the flour, sugar, baking soda, salt, and cinnamon, and stir until well mixed. Add the milk, pumpkin purée, egg yolks, and butter and stir just until combined. Gently fold in the egg whites.

Heat a large skillet over medium-high heat and add oil just to coat the pan. Pour in ⅛ cup batter for each pancake. Do not crowd the pan. Cook the pancakes until golden on both sides and place them on serving plates in the warm oven. Repeat to cook the remaining pancakes. Serve immediately.

Makes 4 large pancakes

Fancy French Toast Club Sandwich

3 eggs
1 cup milk
¼ teaspoon salt
1 teaspoon sifted powdered sugar, plus more for sprinkling
¼ teaspoon vanilla extract
3 raisin bread slices

2 tablespoons butter
Grated or thinly sliced Cheddar cheese to cover 2 slices of bread
2 thin ham slices cut to fit bread
Home Fries (recipe follows)

In a shallow dish, whisk together the eggs, milk, salt, the 1 teaspoon powdered sugar, and the vanilla. Immerse the raisin bread in the egg mixture and let soak.

In a large skillet, melt the butter over medium-high heat and cook the bread until golden brown on the bottom. Turn the bread over to brown the second side. While the bread is cooking, top 2 of the bread slices with the cheese, then the ham. When the bread is golden brown on the second side, stack the bread, ending with the bread slice without ham and cheese.

Transfer the stack to a cutting board and slice diagonally into quarters. Arrange the French toast on a plate with the quarters spaced apart. Sprinkle with powdered sugar. Place some home fries between the quarters and serve immediately.

Makes 1 sandwich

Home Fries

1 pound unpeeled red potatoes
¼ cup bacon fat, butter, or vegetable oil
1 cup finely chopped onion
1 teaspoon minced garlic
Salt and ground white pepper to taste
Paprika to taste (optional)

Cook the potatoes in salted boiling water until almost cooked through, about 15 minutes. Drain and refrigerate for at least 2 to 3 hours, or up to 24 hours. Cut the potatoes into ½-inch dice.

In a large, heavy skillet over medium-high heat, heat the bacon fat, butter, or vegetable oil and sauté the onion and garlic until soft, about 5 minutes. Stir in the potatoes, salt, pepper, and paprika, if using. When the bottom is crisp and browned, turn the mixture using a metal spatula; cook until the potatoes are evenly browned and serve immediately.

Makes 2 servings

Cheese Omelette

Serve with home fries or a muffin.

2 eggs
¼ teaspoon salt
1 tablespoon butter
3 tablespoons grated Cheddar cheese

In a small bowl, lightly beat the eggs and salt together. In a 7-inch omelette pan, melt the butter over medium heat until it sizzles. Pour the eggs into the pan and cook until the eggs are lightly browned on the bottom, tilting the pan and pushing back the edge of the omelette with a spoon to let the uncooked egg run off to the sides. Sprinkle the cheese over the omelette, fold the omelette in half, and serve immediately on a warm plate.

Makes 1 omelette

Apple, Onion, and Cheddar Omelette

3 tablespoons butter
2 tablespoons finely chopped onion
¼ green apple, peeled, cored, and thinly sliced or chopped
2 eggs
¼ teaspoon salt
⅓ cup grated Cheddar cheese

In a small sauté pan or skillet, melt 2 tablespoons of the butter over medium heat and sauté the onion until translucent, about 3 minutes. Add the apple and sauté until soft but not mushy.

In a small bowl, lightly beat the eggs and salt together. In a 7-inch omelette pan, melt the remaining 1 tablespoon butter over medium heat until it sizzles. Pour the eggs into the pan and cook until lightly browned on the bottom, tilting the pan and pushing back the edge of the omelette with a spoon to let the uncooked egg run off to the sides. Sprinkle with the cheese, then the apple mixture. Fold the omelette in half and serve immediately on a warm plate.

Makes 1 omelette

Italian Omelette

1 sweet or hot Italian sausage, cut into ¼-inch crosswise slices
1 tablespoon olive oil
2 tablespoons finely chopped onion
2 tablespoons finely chopped green bell pepper
2 eggs
¼ teaspoon salt
1 tablespoon butter
⅓ cup grated mozzarella or provolone, or Herbed Ricotta (recipe follows)
Grated Parmesan cheese for sprinkling

In a small skillet or sauté pan over medium heat, sauté the sausage until browned and cooked through. Using a slotted spoon, transfer the sausage to paper towels to drain. Pour all the fat out of the pan, add the olive oil, and sauté the onion and green pepper over medium heat until tender, about 5 minutes. Stir in the sausage and heat through. Set aside and keep warm.

In a small bowl, lightly beat the eggs and salt together. In a 7-inch omelette pan over medium heat, melt the butter until it sizzles. Pour the eggs into the pan and cook until lightly browned on the bottom, tilting the pan and pushing back the edge of the omelette with a spoon to let the uncooked egg run off to the sides. Sprinkle or spread with the cheese, then sprinkle with the sausage mixture. Fold the omelette in half, place on a warm plate, sprinkle with Parmesan, and serve immediately.

Makes 1 omelette

Herbed Ricotta: In a blender or food processor, combine ⅓ cup ricotta, ¼ teaspoon minced garlic, and minced fresh oregano and thyme, salt, and pepper to taste until thoroughly blended. Use as an omelette filling, as a sandwich spread, or as a dip for raw vegetables. To store, cover and refrigerate for up to 1 week.

Maine Diner

Wells, Maine

You'll find the Maine Diner on Route 1 as you wind your way up the coast of Maine. A southern Maine landmark for over twenty-five years with its blue-and-white motif, the diner is definitely worth a stop for its home-cooked specialties and terrific service. Brothers Myles and Dick Henry, owners since the early 1980s, offer breakfast all day, a creamy and hearty Seafood Chowder, a "Clam-o-Rama" platter, and their famous Lobster Pie. The diner, which seats about seventy, serves visitors with style and efficiency during the summer (there are days when a meal is turned out every thirty-eight seconds), yet manages to take care of the locals, too. It is one of the few restaurants in the area that stays open year-round. The fertile garden in the back of the diner produces summer vegetables, including peas, tomatoes, eggplants, green beans, and summer squash, that are either served fresh or canned for later use. With the design and spirit of a true diner, the Maine has booth service, a counter and stools, and personable waitresses. Myles says, "We treat the customers like guests in our own home."

Maine Diner

Maine Fried Clams

Seafood Chowder

Lobster Pie

Chicken Pot Pie

Grape-Nuts Custard Pudding

Maine Fried Clams

Delicious served with homemade coleslaw and lemon wedges.

4 eggs, lightly beaten

1 cup milk

Salt and freshly ground pepper to taste

2 cups all-purpose flour

2 cups cornmeal

32 ounces shucked clams, preferably Maine frying clams

6 cups canola oil

In a medium bowl, whisk together the eggs, milk, salt, and pepper. In a shallow dish, combine the flour and cornmeal.

Add one-fourth of the clams to the egg mixture. Drain the clams but do not dry them. Dredge the clams in the flour mixture to coat evenly. Transfer the clams to a large sieve and shake to remove any excess breading. Repeat the process in 3 batches.

In a Dutch oven or a large, heavy pot over high heat, heat the canola oil until almost smoking. Carefully add one-fourth of the clams to the hot oil and fry until golden brown. Using a slotted spoon, remove the clams and drain on paper towels. Repeat the process in 3 batches. Serve the fried clams immediately.

Makes 4 servings

Seafood Chowder

This hearty, creamy chowder won Best Chowder award at the Ogunquit Chowderfest in 1991, 1992, and 1993—a tough contest to win.

One 1-pound lobster
8 ounces clams, preferably Maine steaming clams
8 ounces medium shrimp, peeled and deveined
8 ounces bay scallops
2 potatoes, peeled and cut into ½-inch dice
One 10-ounce can baby clams
½ cup (1 stick) butter
2 cups light cream or half-and-half
2 cups milk
¼ cup minced fresh parsley
1 tablespoon paprika
4 ounces salt pork, finely diced
1 onion, finely diced
Salt and freshly ground pepper to taste
Oyster crackers for serving

Just before cooking, kill the lobster by making an incision in the back of the shell where the chest and tail meet. Plunge the lobster into a large kettle of salted boiling water, cover, and boil for 15 minutes. Using tongs, transfer the lobsters to a bowl and let cool.

In the same pot, boil the clams until they open, about 3 to 5 minutes. Using a slotted spoon, remove the clams and set aside. Add the shrimp and scallops to the pot and cook for 2 minutes. Turn off heat, leaving the shrimp and scallops in the pot.

Holding the lobster upside down on a cutting board, cut away the ribbed membrane as close to the shell as possible with kitchen shears and remove the lobster meat from each shell. Working over a bowl to hold the juices, pick out the meat from the tail, knuckles, and claws. Reserve the green tomalley (liver).

In a medium saucepan, boil the potatoes in salted water to cover until just tender, about 10 minutes; add the potatoes to the soup pot.

Add the lobster meat and tomalley to the pot. Stir in the baby clams and their juice, butter, cream or half-and-half, milk, parsley, and paprika. Shuck the steamer clams, removing the neck sheath, and add them to the pot.

In a medium sauté pan or skillet over medium heat, cook the salt pork for 5 minutes, or until crisp. Stir in the onion and sauté for 5 minutes, or until the onion is translucent. Add the bacon mixture and salt and pepper to the soup pot. Simmer over very low heat just until heated through. Serve the soup with oyster crackers.

Makes 4 to 6 servings

Lobster Pie

Grandmother Woodman's succulent baked lobster is a Maine Diner specialty.

Five 1-pound lobsters
1 cup (2 sticks) butter
2 tablespoons fresh lemon juice
3 cups crushed Ritz Crackers
Fresh parsley sprigs for garnish
Lemon wedges for garnish

Preheat the oven to 425°F. Just before cooking, kill the lobsters by making an incision in the back of the shell where the chest and tail meet. Plunge the lobsters into a kettle of salted boiling water, cover, and boil for 12 minutes. Using tongs, transfer the lobsters to a bowl and let cool.

Holding a lobster upside down on a cutting board, cut away the ribbed membrane as close to the shell as possible with kitchen shears. Remove the lobster meat from each shell. Working over a bowl to hold the juices, pick out the meat from the tail, knuckles, and claws. Reserve the green tomalley (liver). Repeat with the remaining lobsters.

In a large sauté pan or skillet, melt the butter over medium-low heat. Stir in the tomalley and lemon juice; remove from heat. Stir in the crushed crackers and reserved lobster juices; combine thoroughly until the mixture is moist and resembles stuffing.

Divide the lobster meat evenly among 4 individual casseroles. Cover with the cracker mixture, patting it on evenly. Bake in the preheated oven for 10 minutes, or until the top begins to brown. Garnish each lobster pie with parsley and lemon wedges and serve immediately.

Makes 4 servings

Chicken Pot Pie

A diner classic. Be careful: These pies stay hot a long time and it's easy to burn your tongue.

Pastry
2 cups all-purpose flour
¼ teaspoon salt
⅔ cup vegetable shortening
⅓ cup cold water

Filling
1½ pounds boneless, skinless chicken breasts
2 potatoes, peeled and cut into ½-inch dice
1 carrot, peeled and cut into ½-inch dice
½ cup (1 stick) butter, melted
¾ cup unbleached all-purpose flour

2 cups water

2 cups chicken stock (page 228) or canned low-salt chicken broth

½ cup fresh or frozen peas

Salt and freshly ground pepper to taste

Melted butter for brushing

To make the pastry: In a medium bowl, mix the flour and salt together. With a pastry cutter or 2 knives, cut the shortening into the flour and salt until the mixture is the texture of coarse meal. Sprinkle in the water and mix with a fork until the dough forms a mass. Or, process the shortening, flour, and salt in a food processor until the mixture is the texture of coarse meal. Sprinkle in the water and process until the mixture forms a mass. Press into a disk, cover, and refrigerate for at least 30 minutes.

To make the filling: In a large saucepan, combine the chicken breasts and water to cover. Simmer over medium-low heat until the chicken is just firm to the touch. Using a slotted spoon, remove the chicken and set aside.

In a medium saucepan of salted boiling water, cook the potatoes and carrots for 10 minutes, or until the potatoes are tender. Drain the vegetables and set aside.

In large saucepan, melt the butter over low heat and stir in the flour; cook and stir for 5 minutes. Whisk in the water and chicken stock or broth. Add the chicken, potatoes, carrots, peas, salt, and pepper. Cook until thickened. Set aside.

Preheat the oven to 450°F. Lightly butter 6 individual casseroles. On a lightly floured surface, roll the dough out to form a rectangle ¼ inch thick. Cut into 6 circles a little larger than the casseroles.

Divide the filling evenly among the casseroles. Place a pastry circle on top of each casserole, pressing around the outside of the casserole with a wet fork to seal. Cut in steam vents and brush with melted butter. Bake in the preheated oven for 12 minutes, or until the crust is golden brown.

Makes 6 pies

Grape-Nuts Custard Pudding

A traditional New England dessert featured at the Maine Diner.

Grape-Nuts for sprinkling
4 eggs
4 cups milk
½ cup sugar
½ teaspoon vanilla extract
Pinch of salt
¼ teaspoon ground nutmeg
Whipped cream (optional)

Preheat the oven to 325°F. Butter the bottom and sides of an 8-inch square baking dish. Sprinkle in just enough Grape-Nuts to cover the bottom of the dish.

In a medium bowl, beat the eggs. Whisk in the milk, sugar, vanilla extract, salt, and nutmeg. Pour the egg mixture into the baking dish and bake in the preheated oven for 1½ hours, or until the top is golden brown and the center is set. Let cool. Serve with whipped cream, if desired.

Makes 6 servings

Max's Diner

San Francisco, California

Max's Diner is owner Dennis Berkowitz's fantasy of an all-American diner that serves "Everything you always wanted to eat." Big, streamlined, and bustling, Max's serves breakfasts, lunches, and dinners at comfortable booths and a long counter; part of the fun includes coin-operated jukeboxes at the booths, pictures of historic diners on the wall, and complimentary Bazooka bubble gum. The diner's huge menu of unpretentious but excellent food includes towering deli sandwiches, blue plate specials, steaks, poultry, seafood, low-fat dishes, and regular hamburgers or basketfuls of little White Castle–style "sliders." Max's delicious housemade pastries, cakes, pies, ice cream, and cheesecake, famous for their astounding size, are definitely large enough to share.

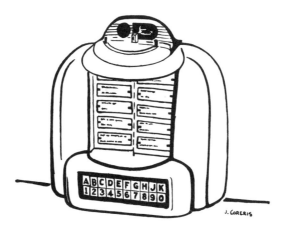

Max's Diner

Baked Cheese Bread with Marinara Sauce

Max's Diner Pot Roast with Red Wine Sauce

Lemon Meringue Pie

Baked Cheese Bread with Marinara Sauce

Marinara Sauce
1 tablespoon olive oil
½ teaspoon minced garlic
2 tomatoes, diced, or 2 cups chopped canned tomatoes
½ cup tomato paste
2 tablespoons dry red wine
¼ teaspoon dried basil
1 tablespoon minced fresh parsley
Salt and freshly ground pepper to taste

Cheese Bread
⅓ cup mayonnaise
¾ cup (3 ounces) grated Parmesan cheese
¼ teaspoon minced garlic
Dash of Tabasco sauce
Pinch of cayenne pepper
Drop of fresh lemon juice
1 sourdough French roll, split in half
Minced fresh parsley for garnish

To make the marinara sauce: In a medium saucepan over medium heat, heat the olive oil and sauté the garlic for 2 minutes. Stir in the tomatoes, tomato paste, red wine, basil, parsley, salt, and pepper. Reduce heat to low and simmer for 30 minutes.

To make the cheese bread: Preheat the oven to 400°F. In a small bowl, combine the mayonnaise, Parmesan cheese, garlic, Tabasco sauce, cayenne, and lemon juice and stir until well blended. Spread the mixture on both halves of the French roll. Place the bread, cut-side up, on a baking sheet and bake in the preheated oven for 20 minutes, or until browned and bubbly. Remove from the oven and slice into 6 to 8 pieces. Sprinkle with parsley and serve with a dish of the marinara sauce for dipping.

Makes 2 servings

Max's Diner Pot Roast with Red Wine Sauce

This dish is pictured on the cover of this book. Serve with mashed potatoes and a fresh vegetable such as green beans, peas, or carrots.

¼ cup beef concentrate

¼ cup tomato paste

Four 2-pound pieces of tri-tip steak, trimmed

⅓ cup olive oil

½ teaspoon dried oregano

½ teaspoon dried basil

1 teaspoon ground pepper

1 teaspoon salt

1½ to 2 cups all-purpose flour for dredging

3 cups dry red wine

1¼ cups beef stock (page 226) or canned low-salt beef broth

4 carrots, peeled and chopped

3 potatoes, peeled and diced

1 celery stalk, chopped

2 bay leaves

Preheat the oven to 400°F. In a small bowl, combine the beef concentrate and tomato paste and stir until well blended. Coat the tri-tips with olive oil, then smear them with the tomato paste mixture. Sprinkle with the oregano, basil, pepper, and salt, then dredge the meat in the flour until thoroughly coated.

Transfer the meat to a Dutch oven or large, heavy casserole, cover, and bake in the preheated oven for 30 minutes. Using a fork, turn the tri-tips over and add the red wine, stock or broth, carrots, potatoes, celery, and bay leaves; stir to dissolve the flour. Cover and bake 1 hour longer, or until the meat is tender. Transfer the meat to a warm platter.

Strain the braising liquid into a saucepan, pressing the juices out of the vegetables with the back of a spoon. Bring the sauce to a simmer over medium heat for several minutes, skimming off any fat that rises. Season to taste. If the sauce is too thin, boil it down rapidly; if too thick, thin it out with spoonfuls of stock or broth. Slice the meat and serve it with the red wine sauce.

Makes 12 servings

Lemon Meringue Pie

The extra-tall meringue on top of this classic pie makes for a dramatic dessert.

Lemon Custard
3 cups sugar
7 tablespoons cornstarch
½ teaspoon salt
3⅜ cups water
9 egg yolks
2½ teaspoons grated lemon zest
4½ tablespoons butter
⅝ cup fresh lemon juice

Meringue
9 egg whites
¼ teaspoon salt
½ teaspoon cream of tartar
⅜ cup sugar

One fully baked 10-inch pie shell (page 233)

To make the lemon custard: In a medium saucepan, combine the sugar, cornstarch, and salt, and stir until well blended. Gradually stir in the water. Bring to a boil over medium heat, stirring constantly. Boil the mixture for 1 minute. Set aside.

In a medium bowl, combine the egg yolks and lemon zest, and beat until pale. Beat a small amount of the hot liquid into the egg yolks. Gradually stir the yolk mixture into the hot mixture in the saucepan. Return the pan to medium heat and stir constantly until thickened, about 20 minutes. Remove from heat and stir in the butter until it melts. Gradually stir in the lemon juice. Pour the custard into the prebaked pie shell; let cool.

To make the meringue: Preheat the oven to 375°F. In a large bowl, beat the egg whites until frothy. Add the salt and cream of tartar and continue beating until soft peaks form. Gradually add the sugar while beating until stiff, glossy peaks form. Spread the meringue on top of the filled pie shell to touch the edges of the crust. Bake for 8 to 10 minutes, or until the meringue turns a light golden brown. Let the pie cool and cut into wedges to serve.

Makes one 10-inch pie; serves 8

Mayfair Diner

Philadelphia, Pennsylvania

A 1956 Mahony (called "the Cadillac of dining cars" and reportedly the longest ever built, at 118½ feet), the Mayfair is a classic diner featuring wholesome food and accommodating service. This Northeast Philadelphia institution draws people twenty-four hours a day with its three-story landmark sign. People line up to get a booth, and the menu changes twice daily because there are so many repeat customers. A diner has been run by the Mulholland family at this location since 1932, when coffee cost five cents a cup and the Mayfair section of Philadelphia was mostly farmland. The diner's classic gleaming stainless-steel facade has been meticulously maintained by Ed, Jack, and Claire Mulholland, who keep the diner's tradition alive. The Mayfair's generous servings of delicious, home-style food keeps three thousand customers on average per day coming into what, according to Jack Mulholland, is basically "a neighborhood place." "But," he says, "other people come and admire the fact that we're still a fifties-style diner—an original one."

Mayfair Diner

Crab Cakes

Old-Fashioned German Potato Salad

Mayfair Diner Dutch Meatballs

Mashed Turnips and Potatoes

Bread Pudding

Crab Cakes

Serve these crab cakes with fresh corn on the cob and a side dish of coleslaw.

6 tablespoons vegetable shortening
2 tablespoons minced onion
¾ cup plus 2 tablespoons all-purpose flour
¼ teaspoon salt
¼ teaspoon dry mustard
¼ teaspoon ground white pepper
1 or 2 drops Tabasco sauce, or to taste
1⅓ cups milk, heated
1 pound fresh lump crabmeat, picked over for pieces of shell and flaked
Flour for dredging
Melted butter for drizzling
Oil for frying

In a medium saucepan over medium heat, melt the vegetable shortening and sauté the onion until translucent, about 5 minutes.

In a small bowl, combine the flour, salt, mustard, and pepper. Stir the flour mixture and Tabasco into the onion mixture and combine thoroughly. Gradually stir in the hot milk and cook until the mixture thickens. Remove from heat and gently fold in the crabmeat in 3 batches.

Let the crab mixture cool slightly. Shape it into patties about ½ inch thick and 2½ inches in diameter. (The mixture should hold together, but it may be moist, so handle gently.) Dredge each crab cake in flour and drizzle on both sides with a little melted butter.

Film a large, well-seasoned cast-iron skillet or a heavy nonstick sauté pan with oil and heat over medium-high heat. Fry the crab cakes 4 minutes on each side. Remove and drain on paper towels. Serve the crab cakes immediately, with extra Tabasco sauce if desired.

Makes 8 to 10 servings, or about 20 crab cakes

Old-Fashioned German Potato Salad

This easy-to-make recipe has evolved over the years from many sources, including Jack Mulholland's Alsatian mother-in-law.

2½ pounds Red Bliss or other red new potatoes, unpeeled
¼ green bell pepper, cored, seeded, and finely diced
1½ celery stalks, finely diced
½ onion, finely diced
¼ teaspoon salt
¼ teaspoon ground pepper
¼ teaspoon celery seed
5 bacon slices, cut into 1-inch squares
½ cup distilled white vinegar
½ cup water, chicken stock (page 228), or canned low-salt chicken broth
1 egg, lightly beaten

In a large pot of salted boiling water, cook the potatoes for 20 minutes, or until tender but still firm. Drain and let cool completely. Peel the potatoes and slice them ¼ inch thick. In a large bowl, combine the potatoes, green pepper, celery, onion, salt, pepper, and celery seed; toss to combine.

In a medium skillet over medium heat, fry the bacon for 5 minutes, or until fairly crisp. Drain on paper towels. Reserve the bacon drippings.

In a small saucepan, combine the vinegar, water or chicken stock or broth, and the reserved bacon drippings; simmer over medium-low heat for 2 or 3 minutes. Pour some of this mixture over the potatoes and gently toss until the liquid is absorbed. Continue gradually pouring the liquid over the potatoes and tossing until they cannot absorb any more. Immediately add the egg and bacon pieces and toss gently. Serve the potato salad warm or at room temperature.

Makes 6 to 8 servings

Mayfair Diner Dutch Meatballs

These meatballs are delicious served with mashed turnips and potatoes.

Meatballs

1 pound lean ground beef

12 ounces ground pork

½ cup finely chopped onion

½ cup finely chopped celery

½ cup dried bread cubes

Beef stock (page 226), veal stock, or canned low-salt beef broth as needed

1 teaspoon minced fresh parsley

½ teaspoon salt

⅛ teaspoon ground pepper

¼ teaspoon Worcestershire sauce

1 egg

¼ cup milk

1 tomato, finely chopped

⅛ teaspoon soy sauce

⅛ teaspoon dry mustard

Pinch of garlic powder

Pinch of ground thyme

Sauce

2 cups chicken stock (page 228) or canned low-salt chicken broth

¼ cup finely chopped celery

¼ cup shredded carrot

4 tablespoons butter

¼ cup all-purpose flour

¼ teaspoon onion salt

⅛ teaspoon ground white pepper

½ teaspoon fresh lemon juice

1 bay leaf

1 teaspoon minced fresh parsley

1 pound wide egg noodles, cooked

In a large bowl, mix all the meatball ingredients just until thoroughly combined; don't overmix. Cover and chill in the refrigerator for 2 to 3 hours before forming into meatballs. Set aside.

Preheat the oven to 325°F. Form the meat mixture into balls and arrange in a single layer in a shallow baking dish. Bake in the preheated oven for 25 minutes. Pour off any fat and bake 10 minutes longer. Set aside.

Meanwhile, to make the sauce: In a medium saucepan, bring the chicken stock or broth to a boil. Add the celery and carrot and boil for 20 minutes.

In a large sauté pan or skillet, melt the butter over low heat and stir in the flour. Cook for 5 minutes, stirring constantly. Whisk in the stock or broth mixture and cook until thickened. Add the onion salt, pepper, lemon juice, bay leaf, and parsley and cook for 5 minutes. Gently add the meatballs to the sauce. Serve the meatballs and sauce over the egg noodles.

Makes 6 to 8 servings

Mashed Turnips and Potatoes

1 bacon slice, or 1 tablespoon butter

2 pounds turnips or rutabagas, peeled and quartered

8 ounces Red Bliss or other red new potatoes, peeled

8 ounces sweet potatoes (not yams), peeled

2 carrots, peeled

⅛ teaspoon salt

⅛ teaspoon ground pepper

If using bacon fat, cook the bacon in a small sauté pan or skillet over medium-low heat until crisp, about 5 minutes. Remove the bacon and reserve for another use; set aside the bacon fat.

In 4 medium saucepans of salted boiling water, cook the turnips or rutabagas, potatoes, sweet potatoes, and carrots separately for 30 to 45 minutes, or until each vegetable is tender. Drain, reserving a little of the cooking water.

Transfer the vegetables to a blender or food processor and purée, in batches if necessary, adding some of the reserved water if needed. Pour into a warm bowl and mix in the bacon fat or butter, salt, and pepper. Serve immediately.

Makes 6 to 8 servings

Bread Pudding

5 cups milk
6 eggs, lightly beaten
¾ cup sugar
Dash of salt
1 teaspoon vanilla extract
½ cup golden raisins (optional)
7 slices firm-textured white bread, cut into fourths
Ground cinnamon for sprinkling

Preheat the oven to 350°F. In a medium bowl, whisk together the milk, eggs, sugar, salt, vanilla extract, and raisins, if using; set aside.

Line a 9-by-13-inch glass baking dish with the bread pieces, overlapping them slightly. Gradually pour the custard mixture over the bread; push the slices back into the liquid and let them soak. Sprinkle liberally with cinnamon.

Place the baking dish in a larger ovenproof pan. Pour water into the pan to 1 inch up the sides of the baking dish. Bake in the preheated oven for 1 to 1½ hours, or until the pudding is set and a knife inserted in the center comes out clean. Serve warm.

Makes 8 to 10 servings

Mels

San Francisco and Los Angeles, California

Mels Drive-In of San Francisco has an unusual and famous history: Mel Weiss and Harold Dobbs built their first drive-in restaurant in 1947, based on ones they had seen in Los Angeles. Soon, fourteen carhops were covering a thirty-thousand-square-foot parking lot. This success led to ten new Mels in Northern California, which reigned until the advent of fast food about twenty years later. Then, Mels began a decline that was to have an amazing turn-around. George Lucas immortalized the historic drive-in in his movie *American Graffiti*—which opened in theaters just as bulldozers razed the last remnants of the original building. The ensuing popularity and nostalgia for the fifties diner led Mel's son Stephen to resurrect Mels. At the grand reopening in 1985, former teenagers who had eaten at the first Mels were eating at the new drive-in with their families, showing their kids a glimpse of the "good old days." Mels' success has spread once again, and there are now three Mels in San Francisco, two in Los Angeles, and full-scale replicas—complete with food service—at the Universal Studios parks in Florida and California. Patrons in San Francisco enjoy Mels classic hamburgers, blue plate specials, sandwiches, pies, and shakes. Nearly everything is made on the premises, and kids' meals are served in a car-shaped box for children to take home.

Mels

American Graffiti Chicken

'57 Ford Omelette

Mel's Deluxe Sundaes

American Graffiti Chicken

Serve with French fries, potato salad, or coleslaw.

2 whole-wheat buns, split
2 boneless, skinless chicken breast halves
½ cup sautéed mushrooms
2 slices Swiss cheese
⅔ cup shredded iceberg lettuce
Sliced tomato, red onion, and pickles
Bacon or grilled onions (optional)
2 to 4 tablespoons mayonnaise

Preheat the broiler. Place the buns, cut-side up, on the broiler pan and toast until golden, about 2 minutes. Set aside.

Arrange the chicken breasts on the broiler pan and broil 6 inches from the heat source for 4 to 5 minutes, then turn and broil on the second side for 3 to 4 minutes, or until springy to the touch.

Transfer the broiled chicken to a large skillet. Top each chicken breast with half of the sautéed mushrooms and a slice of cheese; cover the skillet and cook over medium heat until the cheese melts. Transfer each breast to the bottom half of a toasted bun, top with lettuce, tomato, red onion, and pickles. Add bacon or grilled onions, if desired. Spread 1 or 2 tablespoons mayonnaise on each top bun and serve immediately.

Makes 2 servings

'57 Ford Omelette

2 to 3 eggs
Pinch of salt and freshly ground pepper
1 tablespoon vegetable oil
3 tablespoons finely chopped tomato
1 tablespoon finely chopped green onion
⅓ cup sautéed spinach
1 tablespoon butter
1 tablespoon sour cream
1 teaspoon minced fresh parsley
⅔ cup grilled sliced potatoes
1 orange zest twist and 1 parsley sprig for garnish

In a small bowl, whisk the eggs, salt, and pepper together until well blended. Set aside.

Heat a small sauté pan or skillet over medium heat, add the oil, and cook the tomato, green onion, and spinach until the spinach is wilted. Set aside.

In a 7-inch omelette pan over medium heat, heat the butter and pour in the eggs. When the eggs begin to cook, lift the edges with a spoon to let the uncooked egg run underneath the cooked portion. When the eggs are almost set, spread with the spinach mixture, fold the omelette in half, remove from heat, and place the omelette on a warm plate. Top with the sour cream and sprinkle with parsley. Arrange the grilled potatoes on the plate, garnish with an orange twist and parsley sprig, and serve immediately.

Makes 1 serving

Mel's Deluxe Sundaes

8 tablespoons fudge or butterscotch sauce (page 230 or 228)
4 scoops vanilla ice cream
⅓ cup lightly sweetened whipped cream
Toasted chopped nuts for sprinkling (page 234)
2 maraschino cherries

Pour 2 tablespoons chocolate sauce or butterscotch sauce into each of two 10-ounce sundae goblets. Arrange 2 scoops of vanilla ice cream in each goblet and drizzle 2 more tablespoons of sauce over. Top with half the whipped cream, sprinkle with half the nuts, and crown with a maraschino cherry. Serve immediately.

Makes 2 sundaes

Mickey's Diner

St. Paul, Minnesota

Mickey's Diner, a Jerry O'Mahony diner delivered to St. Paul in 1939, was founded by David "Mickey" Crimmons and John "Bert" Mattson. Listed today on the National Register of Historic Places, the eye-catching red and cream dining car was built in the streamlined Art Deco style. Turning out homemade food like Buttermilk Pancakes, Mulligan Stew, and Bean Soup, the cooks at Mickey's Dining Car use real butter, farm-fresh eggs, and bread baked daily by a St. Paul bakery.

Mickey's Diner

Mickey's Bean Soup

O'Brien Potatoes

Bread Pudding

Mickey's Bean Soup

A cool weather favorite. For an authentic diner experience, serve with saltine crackers.

1½ cups dried Great Northern beans
⅓ cup diced onion
⅓ cup chopped ham
1 ham hock
8 cups water
2 teaspoons liquid smoke (optional)
Salt and freshly ground pepper to taste
Crackers for serving

Rinse and pick over the beans to remove any stones. In a large, heavy pot, combine the beans, onion, ham, liquid smoke, ham hock, and water. Bring to a boil, reduce heat to low, and simmer the soup for 1½ hours, occasionally skimming any foam that rises to the surface. Remove the ham hock and let cool; shred the meat from the bone. Add the shredded ham, optional liquid smoke, salt, and pepper to the soup, mix thoroughly, and simmer for another 30 minutes, or until tender, stirring occasionally. Ladle the soup into bowls and serve with crackers.

Makes 6 servings

O'Brien Potatoes

Serve with scrambled eggs, burgers, or short ribs.

6 potatoes
2 tablespoons vegetable oil
1⅓ cups finely chopped onions
1⅓ cups diced ham
1⅓ cups chopped green bell peppers
Salt and freshly ground pepper to taste

In a large saucepan of salted boiling water, cook the potatoes for 20 minutes, or until tender. Transfer to a plate and let cool completely. Peel the potatoes and cut them into ½-inch cubes or, using a potato peeler, shred them.

In a large sauté pan or skillet over medium heat, heat 1 tablespoon of the oil and add the potatoes. Top with onions, ham, and green peppers. Drizzle the remaining 1 tablespoon oil over the potato mixture and cook until the bottom of the potatoes are crisp and brown. Using a spatula, turn the potato mixture over and brown on the other side. Season with salt and pepper and serve immediately.

Makes 4 servings

Bread Pudding

2 cups milk
3 eggs, beaten
½ cup sugar
⅜ teaspoon salt
2 tablespoons butter
¾ teaspoon vanilla extract
4 slices stale bread, cubed
¾ cup golden raisins
Dash of ground nutmeg
Whipped cream for serving

Preheat the oven to 350°F. In a medium, heavy saucepan, heat the milk over low heat until small bubbles form around the edges of the pan. Remove from heat. Whisk ½ cup of the hot milk into the beaten eggs. Return this mixture to the pan and stir in the sugar, salt, and butter until the butter melts. Stir in the vanilla.

Arrange the cubed bread and raisins in a shallow baking dish. Pour the custard over and let soak for 10 minutes. Sprinkle with nutmeg and place the baking dish in a larger pan. Fill the larger pan with hot water to two-thirds of the way up the sides of the baking dish. Transfer to the preheated oven and bake for 45 to 50 minutes, or until just set. Serve warm, with whipped cream.

Makes 4 to 6 servings

Mother's Restaurant

New Orleans, Louisiana

For over half a century, Mother's Restaurant has specialized in authentic New Orleans home-style cookery, including the most highly rated po' boy sandwich in New Orleans. ("Po' boy" refers to the size of the sandwich, which makes it a good buy for a poor boy.) Mother's is also highly regarded for its breakfasts, plate lunches, fried seafood, Jambalaya, Etouffée, Gumbo, and Bread Pudding—traditional New Orleans fare. The most popular item on the menu is their Black Ham, which is tender and sweet, with a crisp caramelized glaze. Mother's was established in 1938 by Simon A. Landry as a longshoreman's restaurant. Later a popular hangout for off-duty Marines, it was run by the Landry family until 1986, when Jerry Amato, chef and general manager, and his brother and partner John Amato, bought the operation. Today, the unpretentious cafeteria-style restaurant accommodates eighty-five diners at tables and counters and is cluttered with Marine regalia, photographs, placards, testimonials, and other memorabilia.

Mother's Restaurant

Red Beans

Jerry's Jambalaya

Bread Pudding

Red Beans

This is the traditional Monday dish in New Orleans because it uses up Sunday's ham bone and is easy to make on wash day. According to Creole superstition, the person who finds the bay leaf on his or her plate will have good luck.

2 cups dried red kidney beans
1 tablespoon vegetable oil
8 ounces ham, chopped
8 ounces smoked sausage, sliced
1 onion, diced
½ green bell pepper, cored, seeded, and diced
3 or 4 green onions, including some green tops, diced
3 tablespoons minced garlic
1 bay leaf
¼ teaspoon dried thyme
¼ teaspoon salt
⅛ teaspoon ground pepper
4 cups reduced beef stock (page 226)
4 cups chicken stock (page 228) or canned low-salt chicken broth
Cooked rice for serving

Rinse and pick over the beans to remove any stones. Place them in a bowl of cold water to cover and soak overnight. Or, in a large pot over high heat, cover the beans with cold water and bring to a boil. Boil for 1 minute, remove from heat, and cover; set aside for 1 hour.

In a large, heavy pot over medium heat, heat the oil and sauté the ham and sausage for 10 minutes, or until browned. Remove the ham and sausage and set aside; pour off all but 1 tablespoon fat. In the same pot, sauté the onion, green pepper, and green onions for 10 minutes, or until the vegetables are tender.

Add the beans to the pot. Stir in the garlic, bay leaf, thyme, salt, pepper, reduced beef stock, and chicken stock or broth. Increase heat to high and bring the liquid to a boil. Reduce heat to low, cover, and simmer for 1½ to 2 hours, or until the beans are tender and the liquid has thickened. Stir occasionally to prevent sticking. Serve the beans warm or at room temperature over rice.

Makes 8 servings

Jerry's Jambalaya

Jambalaya, a traditional Louisiana Creole dish, is one of the South's greatest contributions to American cooking. Gerard C. Amato won the Rice Council of America and D. H. Holmes Jambalaya Cookoff with this recipe.

4 tablespoons butter
1 cup diced onion
1 cup long-grain rice
3 bay leaves
2 cups chicken stock (page 228) or canned low-salt chicken broth
1 cup sliced smoked sausage
8 ounces boneless, skinless chicken breast
½ cup diced celery
½ cup diced green bell pepper
1 garlic clove, minced
1½ teaspoons minced fresh thyme
1½ teaspoons minced fresh basil
1½ teaspoons minced fresh oregano
¼ teaspoon ground white pepper
¼ teaspoon cayenne pepper, or to taste
¼ cup unbleached all-purpose flour
⅓ cup chopped green onion tops
¾ cup Creole Tomato Sauce (recipe follows)
Salt and freshly ground black pepper to taste

Preheat the oven to 450°F. In medium ovenproof saucepan, melt the butter over low heat and sauté ½ cup of the onion until translucent, about 5 minutes. Stir in the rice, 1 of the bay leaves, and the chicken stock or broth. Raise heat to high and bring the liquid to a boil. Place the saucepan in the preheated oven and bake for 5 to 7 minutes. Remove the saucepan from the oven and set aside; the rice will be about half-cooked.

In a large, heavy pot over medium-low heat, sauté the sausage until browned, about 10 minutes. Using a slotted spoon, transfer the sausage to paper towels to drain. In the fat remaining in the pot, cook the chicken for 8 to 10 minutes, or until it is springy to the touch. Using tongs, remove the chicken, let cool, and cut into cubes.

In the fat remaining in the pan, sauté the onion, celery, green pepper, garlic,

192

thyme, basil, oregano, white pepper, cayenne, and remaining 2 bay leaves for 5 minutes, or until the onion is translucent. Sprinkle the flour over the mixture and sauté 5 minutes longer. Stir in the sausage, chicken, partially cooked rice, green onions, Creole tomato sauce, salt, and pepper. Reduce heat to low and simmer, stirring frequently, for about 30 minutes, or until the rice is tender.

Makes 6 servings

Creole Tomato Sauce

¼ cup olive oil
1 cup minced shallots
6 garlic cloves, minced
1½ teaspoons minced fresh thyme
1½ teaspoons minced fresh oregano
4 teaspoons minced fresh basil
¼ teaspoon ground white pepper
5 pounds ripe tomatoes, peeled, seeded, and diced (page 232)
¼ cup dry red wine
1 teaspoon sugar
Salt and freshly ground pepper to taste

In a medium saucepan over low heat, heat the olive oil and sauté the shallots for 2 minutes. Stir in the garlic, thyme, oregano, basil, and white pepper and sauté until the shallots are translucent, about 2 minutes. Increase heat to high, add the tomatoes, and bring to a boil. Reduce heat to low and stir in the wine, sugar, salt, and pepper. Simmer the sauce for 1 hour. Transfer the sauce to a blender or food processor and purée. Taste and adjust the seasoning if necessary. Serve warm.

Makes 5 to 6 cups

Bread Pudding

Bread pudding is a great dessert for a large party, and this recipe is easily doubled.

10 cups cubed stale bread, preferably French bread
2 tablespoons brandy

3 eggs, beaten

3 cups milk

1½ tablespoons packed brown sugar

1 cup sugar

1½ cups fruit cocktail, in syrup

¼ teaspoon ground nutmeg

1½ tablespoons ground cinnamon

1 tablespoon vanilla extract

½ cup (1 stick) butter, melted

Buttered Brandy Sauce (recipe follows)

Preheat the oven to 350°F. Lightly butter an 8-inch square baking dish.

In a large bowl, combine all the ingredients except the brandy sauce. Mix together until the bread is soaked and broken into small pieces. Pour the bread mixture into the prepared baking dish and bake in the preheated oven for 1½ hours, or until the edges and top of the pudding are browned. Serve the bread pudding hot, warm, or at room temperature, with a little brandy sauce spooned over each serving.

Makes 12 servings

Buttered Brandy Sauce

1 cup clarified butter (page 230)

⅛ teaspoon ground cinnamon

Pinch of ground nutmeg

2 tablespoons packed dark brown sugar

2 tablespoons brandy

In a small saucepan, combine all the ingredients and bring to a boil over medium heat; immediately remove from heat and serve. The sauce may be kept warm in a double boiler over barely simmering water.

Makes about 1 cup

Rosie's Diner

Rockford, Michigan

In 1987, Jerry Berta, a fun-loving sculptor, rescued a 1947 O'Mahony diner named Uncle Bob's from destruction in Flint, Michigan, and moved it to Rockford. He converted it to an art studio and showroom for his ceramic sculptures (many of them of diners!) and the work of his wife, artist Madeline Kaczmarczyk. Although the Diner Store had a sign saying: "No Food, Just Art," a lot of people, attracted by the diner's shape, came looking for a meal. Bert's response? In 1990, he purchased Rosie's—a streamlined 1947 Paramount Diner from Little Ferry, New Jersey—and moved it next door to feed his hungry patrons. (You may remember Rosie's from the Bounty paper towel "quicker picker upper" television ads.) On a busy day, as many as a thousand people have stopped by for "Good Food Served Right." The entire complex, which now includes three restored diners, plus a new diner that Jerry is building himself, and an 18-hole miniature golf course, pulsates with jukebox hits and yards of neon. Berta, who appreciates the "sculptural qualities" of diners, considers his Dinerland "one big art project."

Rosie's Diner

Chuck Wagon Chowder

Rosie's Meatballs

Peanut Butter and Cream Cheese Pie

Chuck Wagon Chowder

4 slices bacon, diced

1 small onion, thinly sliced

Two 17-ounce cans creamed corn

6 potatoes, peeled and cubed

One 12-ounce can evaporated milk

2½ cups hot water

1 tablespoon salt

¼ teaspoon garlic salt

1½ cups (6 ounces) cubed mild Cheddar or Monterey jack cheese

In a medium skillet, cook the bacon over low heat for 5 minutes, or until crisp. Pour off all but 2 tablespoons of the bacon fat and place the pan over medium heat. Sauté the onion for 5 minutes, or until translucent.

Transfer the bacon mixture to a large pot or saucepan over medium heat and stir in the corn, potatoes, milk, water, salt, and garlic salt. Cook the chowder for 30 minutes, stirring occasionally. Just before serving, stir in the cheese until melted.

Makes 4 servings

Rosie's Meatballs

Meatballs

3 pounds lean ground beef

12 ounces bulk sausage meat

30 saltine crackers

3 eggs, beaten

1 teaspoon salt

½ teaspoon ground pepper

1 teaspoon minced garlic

Sauce

3 tablespoons chili powder

2 tablespoons sweet Hungarian paprika

¾ cup packed brown sugar

1 small onion, diced

1 teaspoon minced garlic

3 cups ketchup

2½ cups water

3 tablespoons apple cider vinegar

Preheat the oven to 350°F. In a large bowl, mix all of the meatball ingredients until well blended. Form into 1-inch to 1½-inch meatballs and arrange on a baking sheet. Bake the meatballs in the preheated oven for 20 to 30 minutes, or until lightly browned. Using a slotted spoon, transfer the meatballs to a crockpot or a large, heavy pot.

To make the sauce: In a medium saucepan, combine all the ingredients for the sauce. Cook over low heat, stirring occasionally, until the sugar dissolves. Pour the sauce over the meatballs and cook for 3 hours on a medium setting in the crockpot, or over very low heat in the pot; stir occasionally. Serve warm.

Makes 8 servings

Peanut Butter and Cream Cheese Pie

1 cup heavy (whipping) cream
8 ounces cream cheese at room temperature
¾ cup smooth peanut butter
1 cup sugar
1 Chocolate Crumb Crust (page 229)
Hot fudge for topping (page 230), optional
2 tablespoons chopped peanuts for topping, optional

In a deep bowl, beat the cream until stiff peaks form. In a medium bowl, stir together the cream cheese, peanut butter, and sugar until well blended. Fold in the whipped cream until blended. Pour the peanut butter mixture into the prepared pie shell and spread to even the top. Top the pie with hot fudge and chopped nuts, if desired. Cover with plastic wrap and chill in the refrigerator for at least 2 hours before serving.

Makes one 9-inch pie

Ruthie & Moe's Diner

Cleveland, Ohio

Ruthie and Moe's Diner is really two diners joined together by a kitchen. A glass block wall joins an O'Mahony diner built in 1935 with a 1956 Kullman; Ruthie & Moe's now seats eighty customers at counters and booths. Ruthie and Moe Helman have owned the diner since 1989, and their menu of traditional diner foods features delicious blue plate specials, fresh breads, and house-made desserts. The diner is crowded every day with a wide cross section of Clevelanders (Moe says, "we've got judges, lawyers, and the crooks all eating together"), who enjoy the friendly atmosphere, the counter jukeboxes, and a changing art exhibition by local artists.

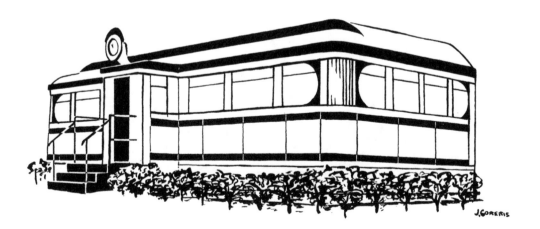

Ruthie & Moe's Diner

Tomato French Onion Soup

Greek Salad with Grilled Chicken Breast and Lemon-Garlic Dressing

Meat Loaf

Apple Pie

Tomato French Onion Soup

½ cup (1 stick) butter

8 onions, thinly sliced

½ cup dry red wine

2 bay leaves

2 tablespoons packed brown sugar

1 teaspoon coarsely ground pepper

4 cups beef stock (page 226) or canned low-salt beef broth

One 16-ounce can diced tomatoes with juice

In a large, heavy pot, melt the butter over very low heat and cook the onions for 20 to 25 minutes, or until golden brown, stirring occasionally. Stir in the wine, bay leaves, brown sugar, and pepper and cook for 5 minutes. Add the broth and tomatoes and cook 45 minutes longer. Remove the bay leaves from the soup and serve.

Makes 6 servings

Greek Salad with Grilled Chicken Breast and Lemon-Garlic Dressing

½ head romaine lettuce

½ head iceberg lettuce

1 small cucumber, peeled and sliced

½ *each* green and red bell pepper, cored, seeded, and thinly sliced

1 tomato, cut into wedges

1 red onion, thinly sliced

Pitted Kalamata olives to taste

2 tablespoons butter at room temperature

1 small garlic clove, pressed

1 boneless, skinless chicken breast, pounded ¼ inch thick
Lemon-Garlic Dressing (recipe follows)

Light a fire in a charcoal grill, or preheat a gas grill or broiler. Make a bed of lettuce on a large platter. Arrange the vegetables attractively on the lettuce. Cover and refrigerate.

In a small bowl, blend the butter and pressed garlic to make garlic butter. Rub the chicken on both sides with the garlic butter. Grill the chicken over a medium-hot fire or under the broiler until browned on both sides and springy to the touch. Slice the chicken diagonally and arrange the slices on top of the salad. Drizzle the salad with some of the dressing and serve.

Makes 2 servings

Lemon-Garlic Dressing

1¼ cups virgin olive oil
⅓ cup fresh lemon juice
1 tablespoon minced garlic
½ teaspoon salt
1 teaspoon ground pepper

In a medium bowl, whisk together all the ingredients. Store, covered, in the refrigerator.

Makes about 1½ cups

Meat Loaf

1½ pounds ground chuck
1 cup fresh bread crumbs
2 eggs, lightly beaten
1 onion, finely diced
1 tablespoon minced fresh parsley

½ green bell pepper, cored, seeded, and finely diced

1 celery stalk, finely diced

1 teaspoon salt

1 teaspoon ground pepper

1 tablespoon Worcestershire sauce

1 teaspoon minced garlic

¼ cup ketchup

Preheat the oven to 350°F. In a large bowl, combine all the ingredients; do not overmix. Pat the meat mixture into a 9-by-5-inch loaf pan and bake in the preheated oven for 1 hour, or until browned and firm to the touch. Let the meat loaf cool for 10 or 15 minutes before slicing.

Makes 6 servings

Apple Pie

Pastry

3 cups all-purpose flour

¼ teaspoon salt

1¼ cups (2¼ sticks) cold butter, cut into small pieces

6 tablespoons ice water

Filling

6 cups sliced tart apples (about 2½ pounds)

2 tablespoons fresh lemon juice

½ teaspoon grated lemon zest

1¼ cups sugar

¼ teaspoon salt

1½ teaspoons ground cinnamon

½ cup all-purpose flour

To make the pastry: Put the flour and salt in a medium bowl and stir. Cut in the butter with a pastry cutter or 2 knives until the mixture resembles coarse meal. Sprinkle in the ice water and stir with a fork until the mixture forms a mass. Or, process the flour, salt, and butter in a food processor until the mixture resembles coarse meal. Add the water and process until the mixture forms a mass. Divide the dough in half, form into 2 flattened balls, wrap in plastic wrap, and refrigerate for at least 30 minutes.

Preheat the oven to 450°F. On a lightly floured board, roll out 1 piece of dough to a ⅛-inch thickness. Fit into a 9-inch pie pan and trim the edges to a 1-inch overhang. Roll out the second piece of dough to a ⅛-inch thickness and trim to an 11-inch circle.

In a large bowl, toss together the apples and lemon juice. Combine the lemon zest, sugar, salt, cinnamon, and flour and sprinkle over the apples. Toss until all the apple slices are well coated. Pour the apples into the prepared pastry shell. Cover with the top crust, cut in some steam vents, and crimp the edges.

Bake the pie in the preheated oven for 10 minutes, then lower the temperature to 350°F and bake 45 minutes longer, or until the crust is golden brown.

Makes one 9-inch pie

Shawmut Diner

New Bedford, Massachusetts

The Shawmut arrived at its present location via a flatbed truck from the Jerry O'Mahony company of Elizabeth, New Jersey, in 1953. It was revitalized by owners Phil and Celeste Paleologos in 1981. The shiny box-shaped diner offers a mingling of tasty Portuguese and American food: Fried Linguica Sausage, Jag (a spicy Cape Verdean dish of rice and lima beans), and a spicy marinated pork dish called Cacoila (pronounced ka-sur-la) are on the menu along with Belgian waffles, omelettes, fresh roast turkey, and sausages with mashed potatoes. The Shawmut serves fish and chips to a crowd on Fridays, a variety of breakfast foods (you can get your eggs with bacon, sausage, ham, linguiça, corned beef hash, or sirloin steak!), and an amazing list of fish, poultry, pork, and beef dishes.

Shawmut Diner

Cacoila

Blackened Chicken with Red Pepper Sauce

Key Lime Pie

Cacoila

This Creole pork stew has Caribbean, French, Portuguese, and Spanish influences. Refrigerate it overnight to improve the flavor and make it easier to remove the excess fat.

5 pounds boneless pork, cut into 1-inch pieces
5 cups dry red wine
5 cups dry white wine
½ cup sweet Hungarian paprika
1 teaspoon ground cinnamon
1 teaspoon red pepper flakes
¼ cup minced garlic
Salt to taste
1 tablespoon granulated onion
¼ cup vegetable oil or bacon fat

In a large bowl, combine all the ingredients except the oil or bacon fat. Cover and refrigerate overnight.

Using a slotted spoon, remove the meat from the marinade, reserving the marinade. In a Dutch oven or large, heavy pot over high heat, heat the oil or bacon fat and brown the meat on all sides, in batches if necessary. Stir in the marinade, reduce the heat to low, cover, and simmer for 1 hour, or until the meat is tender.

Makes 10 to 12 servings

Blackened Chicken with Red Pepper Sauce

Red Pepper Sauce

2 red bell peppers

1 tablespoon dry sherry

Pinch of red pepper flakes

¾ cup sugar

1½ cups water

Juice of ½ lime

Blackening Spice Mixture

¼ cup sweet Hungarian paprika

2 tablespoons garlic powder

1 tablespoon onion powder

1 teaspoon salt

1 teaspoon dried thyme

1 teaspoon dried oregano

4 skinless, boneless chicken breast halves

2 tablespoons vegetable oil

To make the red pepper sauce: Roast the red peppers over an open flame until evenly blackened. Transfer to a paper or plastic bag, close tightly, and let the peppers cool for about 15 minutes. Peel, core, and seed the peppers. Chop them into ¼-inch dice.

In a large, heavy saucepan, combine the sherry, pepper flakes, sugar, water, lime juice, and roasted red peppers. Bring to a boil, reduce heat to low, and simmer for 20 minutes.

Meanwhile, make the blackening spice mixture: In a small bowl, mix all the ingredients until thoroughly combined. Coat each chicken breast with the blackening spice mixture.

In a large, heavy sauté pan or skillet over medium-high heat, heat the vegetable oil and cook the chicken for about 4 minutes, then turn and cook for 2 to 3 minutes on the second side, or until springy to the touch.

Arrange the chicken on each of 4 plates, spoon some red pepper sauce over them, and serve immediately.

Makes 4 servings

Key Lime Pie

One 14-ounce can sweetened condensed milk
5 egg yolks
¾ cup fresh lime juice, preferably from Key limes
One 9-inch graham cracker crust (page 230)
Sweetened whipped cream for topping
Julienned lime zest for garnish

Preheat the oven to 350°F. In a medium bowl, combine the condensed milk, egg yolks, and lime juice and beat until thoroughly blended. Pour the filling into the prepared crust and bake in the preheated oven for 10 minutes. Remove the pie from the oven and let it stand for 10 minutes. Refrigerate until thoroughly chilled, about 2 hours.

Top with whipped cream and garnish with the lime zest. Cut into wedges to serve.

Makes one 9-inch pie; serves 8

Tick Tock Diner

Clifton, New Jersey

In 1994, Tick Tock owners Alex Sgourdos, Steve Nicoles, and Bill Vasilopoulos replaced their modest Musi Diner, originally opened in 1949, with a $1.3 million Kullman-built model. The large diner is built in the 1950s style, with a highly polished stainless-steel, red enamel, and glass-block entrance, and it seats 230 at booths and counter. Displayed in large letters on the clock above the sign outside is the motto "EAT HEAVY." The Tick Tock's extravagant menu is a yard wide and features omelettes, pastries, sandwiches, prime rib, turkey, pasta, seafood, broiled meats, blue plate specials, desserts, and soda fountain specialties.

Tick Tock Diner

Rock Cornish Hens à la Grecque

Spanakopita (Spinach and Cheese Pie)

Braised Lamb with Fresh Greens

Rock Cornish Hens à la Grecque

Sauce

1 cup tomato purée
1 cup chicken stock (page 228) or canned low-salt chicken broth
½ cup dry white wine

4 Rock Cornish hens
½ fresh lemon
Salt and freshly ground white pepper to taste
4 tablespoons vegetable oil or room temperature butter
1 teaspoon dried oregano
¼ cup chicken stock (page 228) or canned low-salt chicken broth
¼ cup dry white wine

To make the sauce: In a small saucepan over high heat, stir together the tomato purée, chicken stock or broth, and wine. Bring the liquid to a boil and cook until reduced by half; set aside.

Preheat the oven to 450°F. Wash the hens and pat them dry with paper towels. Rub the hens with the cut lemon and season the cavities with salt and pepper. Truss the hens with cotton string. Rub vegetable oil or 1 tablespoon of the butter over each hen and sprinkle with oregano.

Arrange the hens breast-side down in a shallow baking pan just large enough to hold them. Bake in the preheated oven for 15 minutes, turn them, and bake 15 minutes longer. Remove the hens from the oven and reduce the oven temperature to 325°F.

Spoon the sauce over the hens and return them to the oven. Bake, basting occasionally with the pan juices, for 20 minutes, or until juices run clear when the inside of a thigh is pierced. Transfer the hens to a heated platter.

Place the baking pan over high heat and add the stock or broth and wine, stirring to scrape up the browned bits on the bottom of the pan. Strain the sauce and spoon it over the hens; serve immediately.

Makes 4 servings

Spanakopita

(Spinach and Cheese Pie)

3 pounds fresh spinach, escarole, or chard, or a combination, stemmed and
    washed but not dried; or five 10-ounce boxes frozen leaf spinach, thawed
    and squeezed dry
10 green onions, white part only, finely chopped
1½ cups minced fresh parsley
1 cup snipped fresh dill, or 4 tablespoons dried dill
12 ounces feta cheese, crumbled (2¼ cups)
8 ounces farmer's or ricotta cheese
8 ounces cream cheese at room temperature
3 tablespoons grated kefalotyri or romano cheese
6 large eggs, beaten
Salt and freshly ground pepper to taste
1 pound filo dough, thawed
1 cup (2 sticks) butter
½ cup olive oil

Preheat the oven to 400°F. If using fresh spinach and/or greens, place in a
large pot, cover, and cook over medium-low heat for 2 to 3 minutes, or until
wilted. Let cool to the touch, then squeeze dry in batches. In a large bowl, mix
together the cooked greens or thawed spinach, green onions, parsley, dill,
cheeses, eggs, salt, and pepper until well blended.

Unwrap the filo dough, place it between sheets of waxed paper, and cover
it with a slightly dampened towel to prevent the dough from drying out.

In a small saucepan, melt the butter over low heat and stir in the olive oil.
Add 3 tablespoons of the butter mixture to the spinach mixture. Brush the
bottom and sides of a 10½-by-15½-inch jelly roll pan with a little of the butter
mixture. Place 1 sheet of filo on the bottom of the pan and brush with some
of the butter mixture. Place 2 sheets of filo in the pan, meeting in the center
and hanging over on opposite sides. Repeat with 2 more sheets, allowing
them to drape over the other 2 sides. Brush with some of the butter mixture.

Tick Tock Diner

Add 4 more sheets of filo in the center of the pan. Brush each with some of the butter mixture.

Spread the spinach mixture evenly into the filo-lined pan. Fold over the overhanging pastry sheets to envelop the filling. Cover the pan with the remaining filo sheets, brushing each with some of the butter mixture. Tuck in the filo all around the sides of the pan to form a neat edge. Brush the top sheet liberally with the butter mixture. Using a sharp, pointed knife, score the top layers of the filo into 5 lengthwise strips and 6 crosswise strips. Gently sprinkle water over the top of the filo.

Bake the pie in the preheated oven for 15 minutes. Reduce the heat to 350°F and bake for an additional 45 minutes, or until golden and puffed. If the pie browns before puffing, cover it loosely with aluminum foil and continue baking until puffed. Let cool for 15 minutes before cutting through the scored pieces. Serve the spanakopita warm or at room temperature.

Makes 30 pieces

Braised Lamb with Fresh Greens

¼ cup olive oil
3 pounds lamb pieces (neck, shoulder chops, or shanks)
2 onions, thinly sliced
One 16-ounce can crushed tomatoes
1 cup water
1 bay leaf
Salt and ground pepper to taste
3 pounds dandelion greens or escarole leaves, cut into thirds crosswise

In a large, heavy pot over medium heat, heat the olive oil and brown the lamb pieces on all sides. Add the onions and sauté until tender but not browned, about 5 minutes. Add the tomatoes, water, and bay leaf and stir to scrape up the browned bits in the bottom of the pot. Cover the pot, reduce the heat to low, and simmer for 1 hour, or until the meat is tender. Season with salt and pepper. Remove the meat from the pot and set it aside.

In a large stockpot of salted boiling water, cook the dandelion greens or escarole for 10 minutes; drain.

Stir the greens into the pot of tomato sauce and place the lamb pieces on top. Cover and cook over medium heat for 20 minutes.

Using a slotted spoon, transfer the lamb to a heated serving platter, making an oval around the edges. Using a slotted spoon, transfer the greens to the platter, mounding them in the center. Skim off all fat from the tomato sauce and spoon the sauce over the lamb and greens. Serve hot.

Makes 6 servings

Victoria Dining Restaurant

Boston, Massachusetts

The only colonial-style diner in Boston, the Victoria Dining Restaurant has successfully adapted to changing food trends and tastes since it opened in the 1920s. It hasn't been called a diner since 1971, when owners Nicholas and Charles Georgenes changed the name to Victoria Restaurant, after their mother, Victoria. (In the 1980s, the name was changed again to Victoria Dining.) The Georgenes' uncle James, with his brothers and some friends and cousins, had a chain of five Worcester diners in the Boston area in the twenties and thirties, but this was the main diner. (Charles Georgenes even worked the bakery part of the chain as a youngster, where his job was pumping jelly into the jelly doughnuts!) Charles and Nicholas (more commonly known as Charlie and Nick) have run Victoria Dining since 1955. In 1975, they added a dining room called Cafe George, styled after an English pub and named for their father. Catering to loyal patrons from nearby communities, Victoria Dining continues to offer the service and friendliness that have always been the hallmark of the Georgenes family. The menu today offers more fresh vegetables and emphasizes fish and chicken over beef, but the high quality is the same. Charles and Nicholas won awards in 1995 from the Epicurean Club of Boston, America's oldest association of professional chefs.

Victoria Dining Restaurant

Braised Lamb Shanks

Chicken Athenian

Veal Parmesan with Fresh Marinara Sauce

Greek Rice Pudding

Braised Lamb Shanks

8 tablespoons olive oil
8 lamb shanks
½ cup all-purpose flour
2 garlic cloves, chopped
1 large white onion, chopped
¼ cup chopped fresh leek (white part only)
3 bay leaves
2 cups tomato paste
4 cups water
Salt and freshly ground pepper to taste
Cooked rice for serving

Preheat the oven to 450°F. In a Dutch oven or a large, heavy pot over medium heat, heat 2 tablespoons of the olive oil and brown the lamb shanks on all sides. Remove the lamb shanks and dust with the flour; set aside.

In the same pot, heat the remaining 6 tablespoons olive oil over low heat and cook the garlic, onion, leek, and bay leaves, stirring occasionally, for 20 minutes, or until the onion starts to brown. Stir in the tomato paste, water, salt, and pepper until thoroughly combined. Purée this mixture in a blender or food processor and return it to the pot. Add the lamb shanks, cover, and bake in the preheated oven for 1½ hours, or until tender. Arrange the lamb shanks over a bed of rice on each of 8 plates and spoon the sauce over.

Makes 8 servings

Chicken Athenian

Serve with butternut squash and mashed potatoes.

¼ cup olive oil

½ cup finely chopped white onion

¼ cup finely chopped celery

4 ounces bulk pork sausage

4 ounces lean ground beef

3 cups dried bread cubes

3 cups chicken stock (page 228) or canned low-salt chicken broth

1 cup chopped cooked broccoli

8 ounces feta cheese, crumbled (1½ cups)

Salt and freshly ground pepper to taste

2 eggs, beaten

Eight 6- to 8-ounce boneless chicken breasts (skin on)

In a large sauté pan or skillet over medium heat, heat the olive oil and cook the onion and celery, stirring occasionally, for 10 minutes, or until the onion is golden brown. Stir in the sausage and ground beef and cook 10 minutes longer, or until the meat is no longer pink; set aside.

In a medium bowl, combine the bread cubes and 1 cup of the chicken stock or broth; soak until the liquid is absorbed. Stir in the broccoli, feta cheese, salt, and pepper. Add the meat mixture and eggs and knead until well blended.

Preheat the oven to 375°F. Stuff each chicken breast evenly under the skin with one-eighth of the meat mixture. Arrange the chicken in a baking dish and bake in the preheated oven for 50 minutes, or until tender.

In a small saucepan over high heat, bring the remaining 2 cups chicken stock or broth to a boil and cook to reduce by half. Taste and adjust the seasoning. Place a stuffed chicken breast on each of 8 plates. Pour some of the reduced liquid over each chicken breast and serve.

Makes 8 servings

Veal Parmesan with Fresh Marinara Sauce

Marinara Sauce

8 tablespoons olive oil

1 cup finely chopped white onion

3 bay leaves

8 pounds tomatoes, peeled, seeded, and coarsely chopped (page 232)

8 fresh basil leaves, minced

½ teaspoon dried oregano

Salt and freshly ground pepper to taste

4 garlic cloves, minced

Eight 3½-ounce boneless veal cutlets

Salt and freshly ground pepper to taste

¾ cup all-purpose flour for dusting

2 eggs, beaten

1 cup milk

2 cups fresh white bread crumbs

2 tablespoons olive oil

1 pound mozzarella cheese, sliced

Cooked pasta for serving

Freshly grated pecorino romano cheese for sprinkling

To make the marinara sauce: In a large saucepan over medium heat, heat 6 tablespoons of the olive oil. Cook the onion and bay leaves, stirring occasionally, for 7 minutes, or until the onions are lightly browned. Stir in the tomatoes and cook until the sauce just comes to a boil, about 15 minutes, occasionally skimming off any foam that rises to the surface. Stir in the basil, oregano, salt, and pepper and reduce heat to a simmer. In a small sauté pan or skillet over medium heat, heat the remaining 2 tablespoons olive oil and cook the garlic for 2 minutes, or until translucent. Stir the garlic into the tomato sauce and remove the sauce from heat.

Preheat the oven to 350°F. Lay each cutlet between 2 pieces of plastic wrap and flatten each cutlet with the flat side of a mallet or the bottom of a heavy bottle until thin. Sprinkle the veal with salt and pepper, then dredge the veal in the flour and shake off the excess.

In a small bowl, whisk together the eggs and milk. Place the bread crumbs in a shallow dish. Dip each veal piece in the egg mixture, then into bread crumbs, to coat evenly.

In a large sauté pan or skillet over medium heat, heat the olive oil and sauté the veal until golden brown on both sides, about 3 minutes per side.

Transfer the cutlets to a baking dish and cover them with a thin layer of marinara sauce. Top with the mozzarella and bake in the preheated oven for 5 minutes, or until the cheese starts to bubble. Serve with pasta, the remaining marinara sauce, and grated cheese for sprinkling.

Makes 8 servings

Greek Rice Pudding

4 cups milk
½ cup long-grain white rice
½ teaspoon salt
½ cup sugar
Grated zest of ½ lemon
Pinch of ground nutmeg
Ground cinnamon for dusting
Whipped cream for garnish (optional)

In a heavy, medium saucepan over low heat, combine the milk, rice, salt, sugar, lemon zest, and nutmeg; cook, stirring frequently, for 40 minutes, or until the rice is soft and creamy. Pour the rice pudding into 8 serving dishes and dust with cinnamon. Refrigerate until cool, garnish with whipped cream if desired, and serve.

Makes 8 servings

BASICS

Applesauce

4 Granny Smith or other tart green apples, peeled and cored
1 cup water
¼ cup sugar
½ teaspoon ground cinnamon

Cut the apples into 1-inch chunks. In a saucepan over medium heat, combine the water and apples. Cover and cook until tender. Stir in the sugar and cinnamon and cook until the sugar dissolves. Using a potato masher, coarsely mash the apples, mixing them into the liquid.

Makes about 6 cups

Artichoke Hearts

8 medium artichokes
1 lemon, cut in half

Cut off the base of the artichokes and break off all the leaves up to the top third; cut off the top with a sharp knife. Trim off all the green with a sharp knife and cut out the choke. Rub all over with the cut lemon. Bring a large pot of water to a boil. Add the artichokes and cook until tender, about 30 minutes. Drain well.

Makes 8 artichoke hearts

Beef Stock

4 pounds sliced meaty beef shanks
2 tablespoons olive oil
1 onion, chopped
1 carrot, peeled and chopped
1 celery stalk, chopped
1 bay leaf
3 fresh parsley sprigs
6 peppercorns
½ cup dry white wine
3 quarts water
½ cup tomato purée

Preheat the oven to 400°F. In a roasting pan, toss the bones with the olive oil. Brown in the preheated oven for 30 to 40 minutes, turning occasionally. Transfer the bones to a stockpot.

Pour the fat out of the roasting pan, add wine, and stir over medium heat to scrape up the browned bits from the bottom of the pan. Pour this liquid into the stockpot. Add the remaining ingredients. Bring to a boil and skim off any foam that rises to the top. Simmer slowly for 3 to 4 hours.

Strain through a sieve into a bowl and refrigerate. Remove any congealed fat that rises to the surface. Cover and store for up to 3 days in the refrigerator. To keep longer, bring to a boil every 3 days, or freeze for up to 3 months.

Makes about 8 cups

Reduced Beef Stock or Broth
Use an unsalted or low-salt stock or broth. Cook over medium heat at a low boil until reduced by about one-third, or until rich and well flavored.

Brown Gravy

Pour pan juices into a 2-cup measuring cup. Skim off and reserve the fat that rises to the top. For 2 cups of gravy (6 to 8 servings), add ¼ cup of the reserved fat to a medium skillet over low heat. Add ¼ cup of flour and stir until browned and frothy. Remove from heat. Add water to the skimmed pan juices to make 2 cups and pour into the roasting pan. Stir to scrape up any browned bits from the bottom of the pan. Stir this liquid into the flour mixture and cook, stirring constantly, over medium heat until the mixture thickens. Season with salt and pepper to taste. Serve warm.

Brownies

4 ounces unsweetened chocolate
½ cup (1 stick) butter
1 teaspoon vanilla extract
2 eggs, lightly beaten
1¼ cups sugar
¼ teaspoon salt
½ cup all-purpose flour

Preheat the oven to 350°F. Grease and flour an 8-inch square baking pan.

In a double boiler over barely simmering water, melt the chocolate and butter, stirring frequently. Remove from heat and let cool completely.

Stir the vanilla, eggs, sugar, and salt into the cooled chocolate mixture; mix well. Stir in the flour until combined. Spread the batter in the prepared pan and bake in the preheated oven for 45 minutes, or until a toothpick inserted in the center comes out clean. Cut into 16 squares to serve.

Makes sixteen 2-inch brownies

Butterscotch Sauce

This sauce keeps for months in the refrigerator.

5 tablespoons unsalted butter
¾ cup packed light brown sugar
¾ cup packed dark brown sugar
1 cup light corn syrup
1 cup heavy (whipping) cream

In a medium saucepan, combine the butter, sugars, and corn syrup. Bring to a rolling boil over high heat, stirring constantly. The mixture will darken a little as it cooks. Stir in the cream and return the mixture to a boil. Reduce heat to a simmer and cook for 2 minutes; remove the pan from heat. Serve warm.

Chicken Stock

About 4 pounds bony chicken pieces (backs and necks)
1 onion, chopped
1 carrot, peeled and chopped
3 celery stalks, chopped
8 fresh parsley sprigs

Put the chicken pieces in a large stockpot. Add water to cover by 1 inch. Bring to a slow boil, occasionally skimming off any foam that rises to the surface. Add the remaining ingredients. Cover the pan, reduce heat to a simmer, and cook for 1 hour, adding water as necessary to keep the ingredients covered. Strain through a sieve into a large bowl and refrigerate. Remove and discard the surface fat that has congealed on top. Store for up to 3 days in the refrigerator. To keep longer, bring to a boil every 3 days, or freeze for up to 3 months.

Makes about 8 cups

Reduced Chicken Stock or Broth
Use an unsalted or low-salt stock or broth. Cook over medium heat at a low boil until reduced by about one-third, or until rich and well flavored.

Chocolate Crumb Crust

1½ cups chocolate wafer crumbs (about 30 wafers)
¼ cup sugar
½ cup (1 stick) butter, melted

Preheat the oven to 350°F. In a medium bowl, combine the crumbs and sugar. Stir in the butter until all the crumbs are moistened. Empty the crumb mixture into the pie plate and press it evenly around the bottom and sides of the plate. Bake in the preheated oven for 8 to 10 minutes, or until set.

Makes one 9-inch pie shell

Chocolate Mousse

7 ounces semisweet chocolate, chopped
4 egg yolks
2 tablespoons sugar
2 teaspoons vanilla extract
1 cup plus 2 tablespoons chilled heavy (whipping) cream

In a double boiler over barely simmering water, melt the chocolate; remove from heat.

In a double boiler over barely simmering water, whisk together the egg yolks, sugar, vanilla extract, and ¼ cup of the cream until the mixture thickens enough to coat a spoon; remove from heat and let cool slightly.

In a deep bowl, beat the remaining ¾ cup plus 2 tablespoons heavy cream until soft peaks form. Combine the egg mixture and chocolate, then gently fold in the whipped cream. Chill the mousse in the refrigerator for at least 4 hours before serving.

Makes about 2½ cups

Clarified Butter

In a heavy saucepan, melt unsalted butter over low heat. Remove the pan from heat and let stand for several minutes. Skim the foam and pour off the clear liquid, leaving the milky solids in the bottom of the pan. Cover and store in the refrigerator indefinitely. When clarified, butter loses about one-fourth of its original volume.

Fudge Sauce

4 ounces semisweet chocolate, chopped
¼ cup unsalted butter
¼ cup heavy (whipping) cream

In a double boiler over barely simmering water, combine the chocolate and butter; stir until melted and smooth. Stir in the cream just until well mixed. Remove from heat, cover to keep warm, and set aside.

Graham Cracker Crust

1⅓ cups graham cracker crumbs
⅓ cup sugar
½ cup (1 stick) unsalted butter, melted

Preheat the oven to 350°F. In a medium bowl, combine all the ingredients and stir until thoroughly blended. Press the mixture into the bottom and sides of a 9-inch pie plate. Bake the crust in the preheated oven for 8 minutes, or until set.

Makes one 9-inch pie shell

Mashed Potatoes

Red or yellow potatoes make creamy purées, while russets, or baking potatoes, make fluffy mashed potatoes. Evaporating the moisture after cooking helps make the potatoes even lighter and fluffier when mashed.

4 russet potatoes, peeled and quartered
¼ to ½ cup hot milk
2 or more tablespoons butter
Salt and freshly ground pepper to taste

Put the potatoes in a large saucepan with lightly salted water to cover; bring to a boil. Reduce heat, cover, and simmer for 15 to 20 minutes, or until the potatoes are tender. Drain the potatoes and return them to the pan. Place over low heat and shake the pan for a few seconds to dry the potatoes. Place the potatoes in a warm bowl and mash them with a potato masher, or force them through a ricer into a warm bowl. Stir in the milk and butter until the butter is melted. Season with salt and pepper and serve immediately.

Makes 4 servings

Pancakes

1 cup all-purpose flour
3 teaspoons baking powder
1 tablespoon sugar

½ teaspoon salt
1 egg, lightly beaten
1 cup milk
2 tablespoons vegetable oil or melted butter

In a medium bowl, combine the flour, baking powder, sugar, and salt and mix to blend. In a small bowl, beat together the egg, milk, and oil or melted butter. Stir the milk mixture into the flour mixture just until combined; the batter may still be lumpy. Let the batter stand for 10 minutes.

Heat a griddle or large skillet over medium heat and oil it lightly. Drop the batter by heaping tablespoons and cook until bubbles appear evenly on the surface, about 1 minute. Turn and cook for 1 minute on the other side, or until golden.

Makes about eight 4-inch pancakes

Peeling and Seeding Tomatoes

Cut out the cores of the tomatoes and cut an X in the opposite end. Drop the tomatoes into a pot of rapidly boiling water for 10 seconds, or until the skin by the X peels away slightly. Drain and run cold water over the tomatoes; the skin should slip off easily. To seed, cut the tomatoes in half crosswise, hold each half upside down over the sink, and gently squeeze and shake to remove the seeds.

Pie Pastry

½ cup (1 stick) cold butter, cut into small pieces
1½ cups all-purpose flour
¼ teaspoon salt
3 to 4 tablespoons cold water

Basics

In a medium bowl, cut the butter into the flour and salt using a pastry cutter or 2 knives until the mixture is the texture of coarse meal. Sprinkle in the water and mix with a fork until the mixture forms a mass. Or, process the flour, salt, and butter in a food processor until the mixture is the texture of coarse meal. Add the water and pulse until the mixture forms a mass. Press the dough into a flat dish. Cover in plastic wrap and refrigerate for at least 30 minutes before rolling out.

Makes dough for one 8- to 10-inch pie shell

Baked Pie Shell

Preheat the oven to 375°F. Roll the chilled dough out on a lightly floured surface to form a circle 2 inches larger than the pie plate. Fit it into the bottom and sides of a 9-inch pie plate. Trim the dough, leaving a 1-inch overhang; crimp the edges. Prick the bottom of the pastry with a fork and line it with aluminum foil. Fill the plate with pie weights or dried beans and bake in the preheated oven for 8 minutes. Remove the foil and weights and bake until the pastry is golden brown, 10 to 13 minutes. Set aside to cool.

Rendering Chicken Fat

Remove all large pieces of fat from a chicken and place them in the top of a double boiler over barely simmering water. Cook until the fat becomes liquid. Remove from heat and strain through a fine sieve. Let cool and refrigerate or freeze until ready to use. Or, use the congealed fat from chilled chicken stock.

Roasted Peppers

Char peppers over a gas flame or under a preheated broiler until the skin is blackened all over. Using tongs, transfer the peppers to a paper or plastic bag, close it, and let the peppers cool for 10 to 15 minutes. Remove from the bag, peel off the skin with your fingers or a small sharp knife, and core and seed the peppers.

Toasted Nuts

Toast nuts on a baking sheet in a preheated 350°F oven for 8 to 10 minutes, or until very lightly browned, stirring once. Toasted nuts may be stored in an airtight container in the refrigerator or freezer.

Toasted Salted Pecans

Spray pecan halves lightly with cooking spray and turn to coat. Toast on a baking sheet in a preheated 350°F oven for 5 to 8 minutes, or until very lightly browned. Pour into a bowl, sprinkle lightly with salt, and toss to coat.

CONVERSION CHARTS

Weight Measurements

Standard U.S.	Ounces	Metric
1 ounce	1	30 g
¼ lb	4	125 g
½ lb	8	250 g
1 lb	16	500 g
1½ lb	24	750 g
2 lb	32	1 kg
2½ lb	40	1.25 kg
3 lb	48	1.5 kg

Volume Measurements

Standard U.S.	Fluid Ounces	Metric
1 T	½	15 ml
2 T	1	30 ml
3 T	1½	45 ml
¼ cup (4 T)	2	60 ml
6 T	3	90 ml
½ cup (8 T)	4	125 ml
1 cup	8	250 ml
1 pint (2 cups)	16	500 ml
4 cups	32	1 L

Oven Temperatures

Fahrenheit	Celsius
300°	150°
325°	165°
350°	180°
375°	190°
400°	200°
425°	220°
450°	230°

Conversion Factors

Ounces to grams: Multiply the ounce figure by 28.3 to get the number of grams.

Pounds to grams: Multiply the pound figure by 453.59 to get the number of grams.

Pounds to kilograms: Multiply the pound figure by 0.45 to get the number of kilograms.

Ounces to milliliters: Multiply the ounce figure by 30 to get the number of milliliters.

Cups to liters: Multiply the cup figure by 0.24 to get the number of liters.

Fahrenheit to Celsius: Subtract 32 from the Fahrenheit figure, multiply by 5, then divide by 9 to get the Celsius figure.

LIST OF CONTRIBUTORS

A-1 Diner
3 Bridge Street
Gardiner, ME 04345
(207) 582-4804

American City Diner
5532 Connecticut Ave. N.W.
Washington, D.C. 20015
(202) 244-1949

Bette's Oceanview Diner
1807A Fourth Street
Berkeley, CA 94710
(510) 644-3230

Boogie's Diner
534 East Cooper
Aspen, CO 81611
(970) 925-6610

Bubba's Diner
566 San Anselmo Avenue
San Anselmo, CA 94960
(415) 459-6862

Buckhead Diner
3073 Piedmont Road
Atlanta, Georgia 30305
(404) 262-3336

Camp Washington Chili
Hopple and Colerain
Cincinnati, OH 45225
(513) 541-0061

Clarksville Diner
504 Heivly Street
Decorah, IA 52101
(319) 382-4330

The Corvette Diner
3946 Fifth Avenue
San Diego, CA 92103
(619) 542-1001

Country Club Restaurant and Pastry Shop
1717 Cottman Avenue
Philadelphia, PA 19111
(215) 722-0500

Crown Candy Kitchen
1401 St. Louis Avenue
St. Louis, MO 63106
(314) 621-9650

Daddy Maxwell's
150 Elkhorn Road
Williams Bay, WI 53191
(414) 245-5757

The Diner
6476 Washington Street
Yountville, CA 94599
(707) 944-2626

Dutch Kitchen Restaurant
Route 61
Frackville, PA 17931
(717) 874-3265

11th Street Diner
11th Street and
Washington Avenue
Miami Beach, FL 33139
(305) 534-6373

Empire Diner
210 Tenth Avenue
New York, NY 10011
(212) 243-2736

4th Street Diner
184 Admiral Kalbfus Road
Newport, RI 02840
(401) 847-2069

Highland Park Diner
960 South Clinton Avenue
Rochester, NY 14620
(716) 461-5040

Jigger's Diner
145 Main Street
East Greenwich, RI 02818
(401) 884-5388

Maine Diner
Route 1
Wells, ME 04090
(207) 646-4441

Max's Diner
311 Third Street
San Francisco, CA 94107
(415) 546-6297

Mayfair Diner
7373 Frankford Avenue
Philadelphia, PA 19136
(215) 624-8886

Mels
2165 Lombard Street
San Francisco, CA 94123
(415) 921-3039

3355 Geary Boulevard
San Francisco, CA 94118
(415) 387-2244

14846 Ventura Boulevard
Sherman Oaks, CA 91403
(818) 990-6357

19964 Ventura Boulevard
Woodland Hills, CA 91364
(818) 348-6357

Mickey's Diner
Ninth and St. Peter Streets
St. Paul, MN 55116
(612) 698-0259

Mother's Restaurant
401 Poydras Street
New Orleans, LA 70130
(504) 523-9656

Rosie's Diner
4500 14 Mile Road
Rockford, MI 49341
(616) 866-3663

Ruthie & Moe's Diner
4002 Prospect Avenue
Cleveland, OH 44103
(216) 431-8063

Shawmut Diner
943 Shawmut Avenue
New Bedford, MA 02746
(508) 993-3073

Tick Tock Diner
281 Allwood Road
Clifton, NJ 07012
(201) 777-0511

Victoria Dining Restaurant
1024 Massachusetts Avenue
Boston, MA 02118
(617) 442-5965

List of Contributors

ACKNOWLEDGMENTS

I would like to thank the many people who made this volume possible.

The Cookbook

My gratitude to the diner owners and cooks who generously contributed recipes to the cookbook: Michael Giberson, Jeffrey Gildenhorn, Brenda Remchuck, Bette Kroening, Bernie Mysior, Boogie Weinglass, Beth and Steve Simmons, Peter Kaiser, John and Antigone Johnson, Gordon C. Tindall, David Cohn, Tim Mavrakos, Simone and Noel Perloff, Andy Karandzieff, Jeanette Maxwell, Cassandra Mitchell, John Morgan, Ray and Steve Schnitzer, Jack Doenias, Mitchell R. Woo, Tish Warner, Bob Malley, Carol Shriner, Miles Henry, Dennis Berkowitz, Terry Judkins, Jack Mulholland, Eric Mattson, Jerry Amato, Jerry Berta, Ruthie and Moe Helman, Phil and Celeste Paleologos, Alex Sgourdo and Bill Vasilopoulos, Nicholas and Charles Georgenes. Special thanks to Phil Paleologos for allowing me to reprint selections from his "Diner Talk" and to Max's Diner in San Francisco for providing the setting for the cover photograph.

I received an education about diners from Richard J. S. Gutman's *American Diner Then and Now* (HarperPerennial), Gerd Kittel's *Diners People and Places* (Thames and Hudson), and Randy Garbin's quarterly publication, *Roadside*.

I particularly thank Carolyn Miller once again for her thoughtful editing. Many thanks to Eric Liebau, Ned Waring, Tim Forney, Sharilyn Hovind, Jim Armstrong, Steve Patterson, and the rest of the staff at Menus and Music.

Tom Kamegai and Michael Osborne deserve thanks for their design and enthusiastic support of this project. Thanks to John Coreris for the architectural illustrations of diners and to photographer Mark McLane and food stylist Danielle Salvo for the cover photograph.

The Music

I will be forever grateful to Bill Schrey for making the recording a dream come true and for making the project fun from start to finish. Special thanks to recording and mixing engineer Craig Silvey and assistant engineer Chis Heynes at Toast Studio, San Francisco. Thanks to Gary Clayton for bringing us all together. Once again, thanks to George Horn for the digital mastering.

Executive Producer: Sharon O'Connor
Produced by Bill Schrey and Sharon O'Connor
©℗ Menus and Music Productions, Inc.

Bill Schrey: Guitar, background vocals, hand claps, horn arrangements
Rich Kuhns: Piano, organ, glockenspiel
Scott Fuller: Piano, vibes, fingersnaps, hand claps
Rich Girard: Electric bass, acoustic bass, hand claps
Billy Lee Lewis: Drums
Kenny "Blue" Ray: Guitar on "Johnny B. Goode" and "Rock and Roll Music"
Armen Boyd: Horn arrangements and tenor and baritone saxophones
Steve Stanley: Trumpet and flugelhorn
Nathan Rubin: Violin
John Tenney: String arrangements and violin
Sharon O'Connor: Cello and hand claps
Larry Batiste: Vocals on "Shake Rattle & Roll," "Blueberry Hill," "Tutti Frutti,"
    "Searchin'," "Rock and Roll Music"
Jeanie Tracy: Vocals on "My Guy"
Tony Lindsay: Vocals on "You Send Me," "But It's Alright," "My Girl,"
    "Mustang Sally," "Johnny B. Goode"
Keta Bill: Vocals on "Please Mr. Postman," "Heat Wave,"
    "Where Did Our Love Go?"
Chuck Wansley: Vocals on "Ooo Baby Baby," "Shop Around,"
Kathy Kennedy: Background vocals on "Please Mr. Postman," Heat Wave,"
    "Mustang Sally," "Where Did Our Love Go?"

As always, to my diner girls, Claire and Caitlin, and my husband, John, for their love.

INDEX

Index

Index

Index

Sharon O'Connor is a musician, author, and cook. She also is the founder of the San Francisco String Quartet and creator of the *Menus and Music* series, which combines her love of music and food. *Rock & Roll Diner* is the tenth volume in her series of cookbooks with musical recordings.